Inti ma cies

The Architecture of Youssef Tohme

Karine Dana and Sebastian Redecke

Intimacies

The Architecture of Youssef Tohme

Birkhäuser

Basel

Layout, Cover Design and Typesetting
Silke Nalbach, Mannheim

Editorial Supervision and Project Management
Henriette Mueller-Stahl, Berlin

Translation
French-English (all texts except for pp. 34–47, 72–87, 126–165 and 192–201)
Garry White, Paris

Translation
German-English (pp. 34–47, 72–87, 126–165 and 192–201)
Julian Reisenberger, Weimar

Copy Editing
Michael Wachholz, Berlin

Production
Amelie Solbrig, Berlin

Lithography
LVD Gesellschaft für Datenverarbeitung mbH, Berlin

Paper
Magno Natural, 140 g/m²

Printing
Grafisches Centrum Cuno GmbH & Co. KG, Calbe (Saale)

Library of Congress Control Number: 2021951269

Bibliographic information published by the German National Library
The German National Library lists this publication in the Deutsche Nationalbibliografie; detailed bibliographic data are available on the Internet at http://dnb.dnb.de.

ISBN 978-3-0356-2254-6

P.O. Box 44, 4009 Basel, Switzerland
Part of Walter de Gruyter GmbH, Berlin/Boston

9 8 7 6 5 4 3 2 1 www.birkhauser.com

Table of Contents

6 **Villa SC**
Akoura, Lebanon
2010-2013

18 **Villa T**
Kornet Chehouane, Lebanon
2008-2014

34 **USJ Innovation, Economy and Sports Campus**
Beirut, Lebanon
2004-2012

48 **Ilot sur le Parc**
Marseille, France
2019-ongoing

56 **A599 Apartment Building**
Ashrafieh, Beirut, Lebanon
2013-2019

72 **MARe—Muzeul de Artă Recentă**
Bucharest, Romania
2013-2018

88 Conversation between Youssef Tohme and Karine Dana

126 **Villa M**
Kornet Chehouane, Lebanon
2015-2018

140 **Villa VR**
Ajaltoun, Lebanon
2011-2016

156 **Brazza District**
Bordeaux, France
2012-2030

166 **Quartier Bruneseau**
Paris, France
2018-ongoing

178 **BLF Disaster Center**
Ghazir, Lebanon
2013-2020

192 **Kalani Resort**
Halat, Lebanon
2012-2017

202 Project Information

205 French Version of the Conversation between Youssef Tohme and Karine Dana/
Version originale de la conversation entre Youssef Tohme et Karine Dana

214 Acknowledgements
215 About the Authors
215 About the Architect
216 Illustration Credits

Villa SC

Akoura, Lebanon
2010-2013

Perched on a cliff edge, at an altitude of 1,500 metres, this house establishes an extreme and direct relationship with the mountains. This palpable confrontation incites the architect to conceive this dwelling as a place to capture the senses, a landscape amplifier.

From the outside, the Villa SC resembles a simple dry-stack basalt stone wall.

The story of the project begins in Beirut, at Youssef Tohme's firm, when the client came to visit him to talk about his desire to build a house near the village of Akoura, some 60 kilometres from Byblos, for him and his daughter. Rather similar in temperament, the two men understood each other quickly. Formerly a businessman, Mr Sc. needed to get away from the city. He needed to get away from Beirut. He had known this area of Mount Lebanon since he was a child and now wished to move there, to live on an isolated piece of land he owned and become a mountain guide. It was by observing Mr Sc. as he moved—barely touching the ground and radiating such a special energy—that the architect determined the elements that would serve as the foundations of his proposal: to build a space of silence where all the senses can be simultaneously awakened. Trusting in this extremely precise feeling he had in relation to his client, the architect therefore sought to build the envelope that would protect the latter and enhance his relationship with the territory. The existing site is stunning in terms of its sensory power. Left totally open and unfenced, it is surrounded by very rich flora and fauna: robust apple trees, medicinal and aromatic plants, birds of prey, hyenas and sounds of wildlife. But how does one insert oneself into such a territory? To answer this question, the architect sought to

Mass plan

imagine architecture as a pure potential for exchange between man and the outside world. Thus, viewed from its surroundings, the Villa SC is a troubling presence. It doesn't project any image; all that one perceives is a low rampart and pleasant-looking masonry, dry-built using massive basalt stones from the Beka valley. Seen from the side, this unfolded wall with very few apertures is an enigma. The heavy stones are visibly mounted with great care, without the use of bonding, but one can feel that they are not just resting on top of each other. Their heaviness seems to be supported. The west side of the house reveals a double concrete wall, openly presented as such. The excessive aspect of the project starts here: the contrast between this gallant low wall and the interior space it contains is enormous. The intensity of the latter is in fact amplified by its relationship to the mountain, which seems to be sucked into the house. The phenomenon of surprise seems to be reversed. It is due to the fact that when you enter, what is outside can seem even more vast. This disparity is all the more emphatic as the plan is composed around a strong, classical and highly structuring figure: a U-shape organised around a patio open on three sides and bordered by a terrace overlooking the valley and protected by a cantilever. The villa is composed of two bedrooms in one wing, and a kitchen-living room-library space in the other. Very precisely positioned and oriented, the lateral views from the living room do not frame the road but the upper part of the mountain as if to detach the viewer's vision from what is trivial in the environment. Similarly, in the bedrooms, the visual relationships with the mountainsides, the sky or the central space are carefully framed. In this way, the Villa SC seems to function like a camera, a camera lucida from which the territory is captured in all its sensitivity. The patio, with its earthy and uneven ground, opens onto the rocky landscape to the east and to the sweep of the valley to the west. An open-air room containing a fireplace absorbs the sensation of emptiness. The cantilevered concrete roof acts as a sound amplifier in addition to providing protection against the rain, which is frequent at high altitudes. The sound of a river below, whereas inaudible around the villa, reverberates when one walks under the roof and diminishes as one approaches the cliff edge. Finally, the terrace, which is free of railings, is set on the brink of the very steep slope, flush with the break in the ground. This terrace places the individual in a situation of levitation but also envelopes them in an inhabited space.

This feeling of calm and this amplification of the landscape were achieved thanks to a construction process that was adapted to the requirements of the project. As the setting is so far away from Beirut and even from any village, this was not a straightforward matter: no company qualified to work with rough concrete and large spans accepted to travel to such a remote site. How then was it possible to preserve the sensitivity of the project when the local workers' tools, methodology—they were used to covering concrete and laying out the stones systematically—and very perception of the material were so different?

In this project as in all the others, the structure and its texture—honed in terms of their tension and expressiveness—signify the architecture and signify Lebanon. The office therefore had to introduce the village craftsmen to a different construction culture. The architects then adapted to what was possible to do but they also assisted the workers in implementing these methods. In particular, they used the reference of the agricultural retaining walls found in the

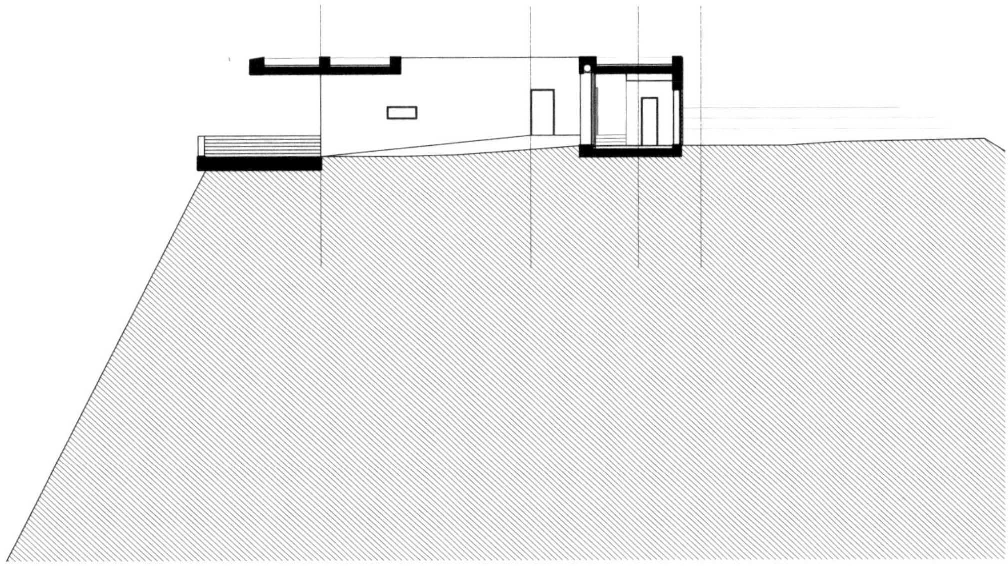

Section

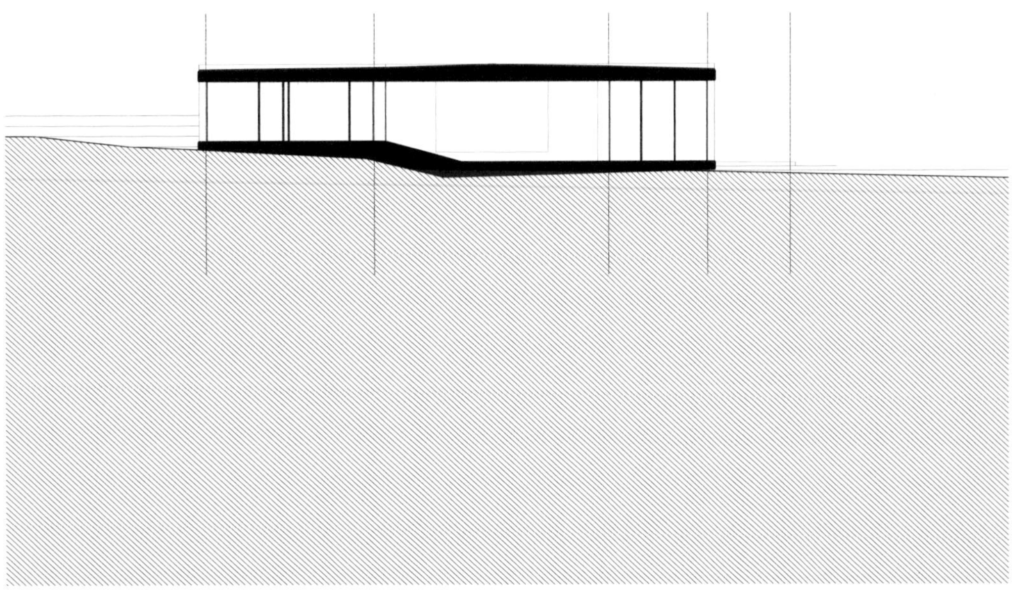

West elevation

Next page: **View from the large terrace sheltered by a cantilever and opening onto the interior spaces facing the great void of the valley**

Emerging calmly from the site, the Villa SC seems to be part of the mountain.

neighbouring valleys to explain the desired method of assembling of the dry stones. They chose the formwork wood to be used for the floors, the 4-metre-high double walls, the floors and ceilings, and the cantilever. Thanks to this involvement in the construction process, the firm was able to achieve the desired refinement, dealing with the technical difficulties encountered, but also with the harshness of the climate and access constraints.

For YTAA, the quality of the work, the clear definition of the surfaces, their softness or intended unevenness, and the constructive legibility constitute a way of establishing links and creating very specific relationships with the body: spacing out points of view or drawing them closer, amplifying vibrations, directing the gaze, encouraging contact, favouring forms of seating and appropriation. In this way, quite subtly, the structure and construction process shape and determine ways of being in the world.

Karine Dana

The Villa SC is organised in a U-shape around a patio open on three sides, bordered by a terrace overlooking the void.

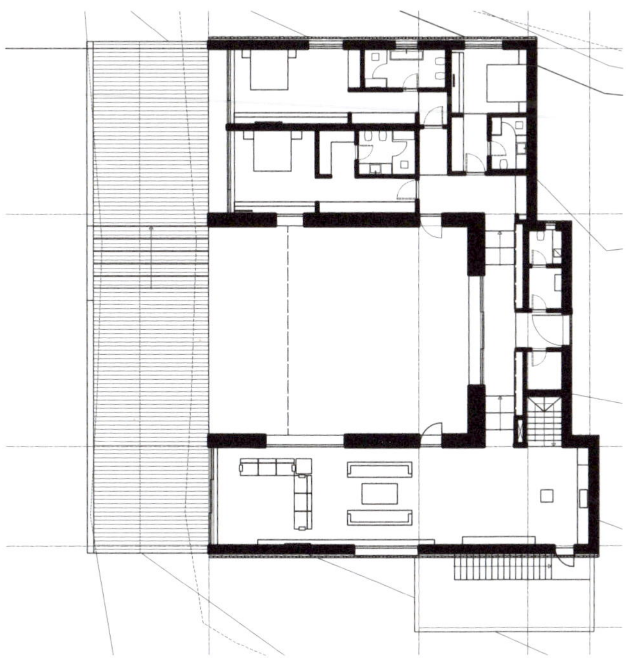

Ground floor plan

Next page: View of the long bookcase fitted along a double wall in rough concrete into which a low window is set

Villa T

Kornet Chehouane, Lebanon
2008-2014

For the design of this anti-villa, the architect moved away from the very idea of a house in order to imagine a living space without beginning or end, without borders or limits, as can fundamentally be the condition of any landscape.

Entrance to the Villa T by way of the gently sloping roof

Inserted in a dense pine forest on the hillside, on the heights of Kornet Chehouane, overlooking Beirut and the sea, Villa T is a very precise composition of expansive, flowing, sloping horizontal surfaces designed to embark the inhabitant on a rare daily adventure: the experience of openness. To understand the open nature of this villa and the astonishing uses that it inspires, one must go back to its origins. In 2007, when Mr. and Mrs. T. approached Youssef Tohme, they wished to build three houses on their family land: one for themselves and one for each of their two children. In response to this request, in itself quite common in Lebanon, the architect envisioned a single setting and a single intention. Above all, he was mindful of preserving this precious site and the tree species it contains. Delicately occupying the slope of the natural terrain, the parents' house was to be positioned between the two children's houses, one above and the other below. The latter was not built in the end. Thus, on this territory that has come under stress due to rushed metropolitan transformations in the middle mountains encircling Beirut following the displacement of populations during the war, peri-urbanisation, foreign investment or the construction of holiday resorts, the architect imagines nothing more than interconnected grounds, inhabited and traversed by the landscape.
He designed a raw concrete structure, some of whose surfaces are cantilevered, while others are to be wandered over, walked along, penetrated or climbed. Thus, Villa T was conceived through a process of subtracting everything with the potential to block, enclose or stop the gaze or movement. It is almost devoid of vertical bearing elements, its floor extensions have no edges, and the clearance of its corners and the opening of its large façade, which extends over 50 metres, efface the boundaries between inside and outside. It does not establish frontality with the landscape, but multiple, angled views because it does not frame anything and thus forges more dynamic relations with the territory. Its main spaces—living rooms, dining room, gallery and bedrooms—are distributed without any hierarchy. Barely emerging from the hill, the villa does not seem to project any formal image. Most strikingly, it does not present an entrance, or rather, it presents several. The villa can be accessed from the monumental car park to the northwest, from the swimming pool in the extension of the house built above, from the corner living room positioned halfway up the garden, or from below, by following the long ramp that winds past the living rooms and up onto the roof. For the architect, the house as a whole is an "entrance", a beginning. What does a door mean in Lebanon? This question, which in turn prompts that of the sign and identity, is fundamental to the architect's thinking. By deconstructing the codes of the bourgeois house and the luxury villa, by inviting users to construct their own relationships to the world, to constantly shift position rather than settle in one spot, to live in movement, Youssef Tohme subverts the highly powerful system of belonging and representation in Lebanon. Thus, the landscape, the topography, the trees, the clouds, the open horizon and the sea are fully part of the project, whereas, around the almost invisible house, five-storey buildings with almost no views or openings pile up on top of each other on deforested land. Through the sense of spatial freedom that emerges from this operation, the architect continues to question the meaning of architecture in Lebanon, which,

Next page: **Propped up against the hill, the Villa T opens onto the bay of Beirut and the wider landscape.**

Composed of interconnected concrete floors and following the natural slope of the terrain, the Villa T merges into a pine forest.

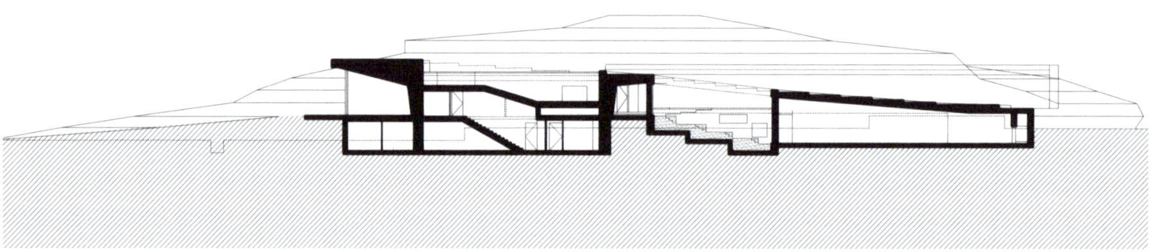

Section

View of the construction phase showing the shoring structures

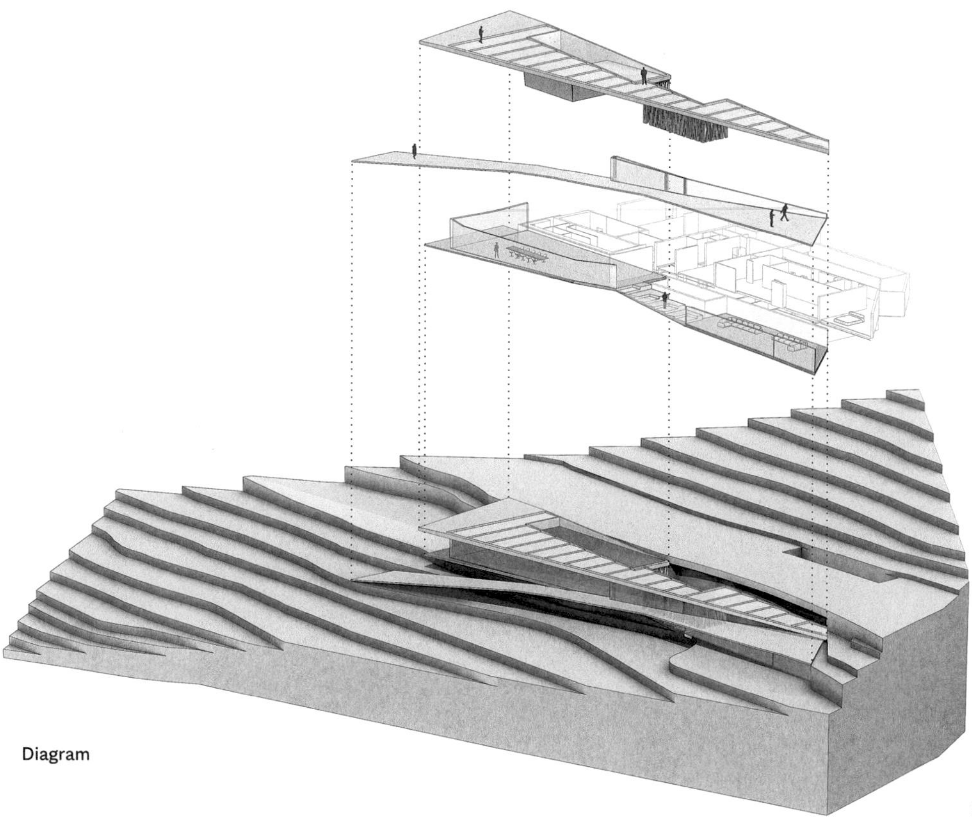

Diagram

Next page: **Shot of the largely open interior space overlooking an atrium offering a scrolling view of the landscape**

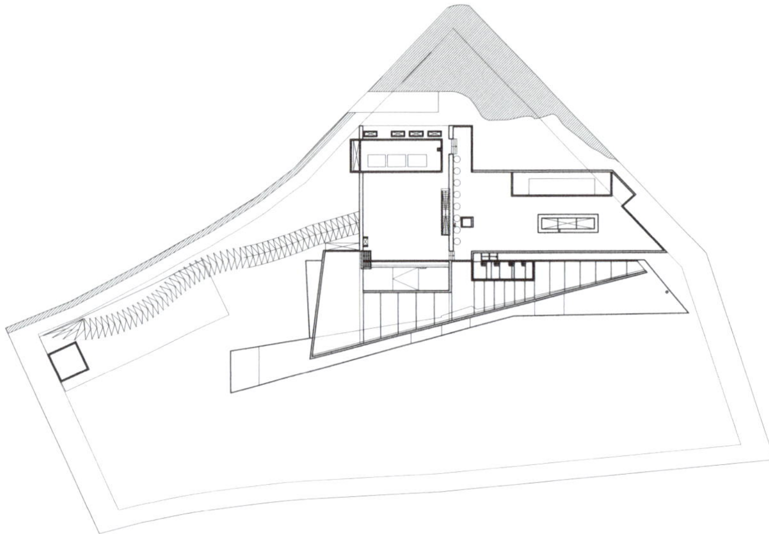

Mass plan

Roof plan

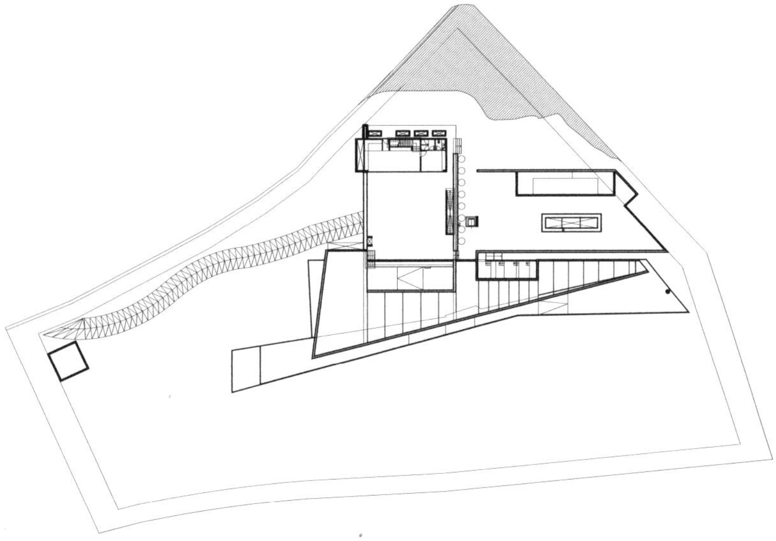

1st floor plan

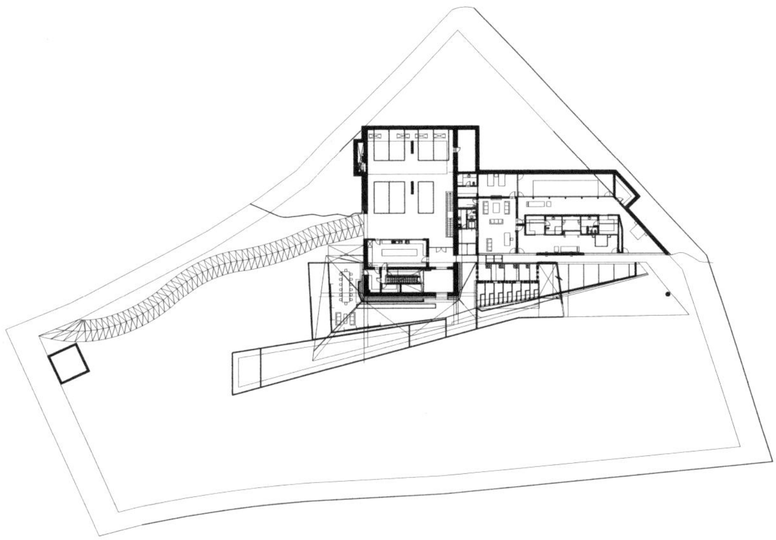

Ground floor plan

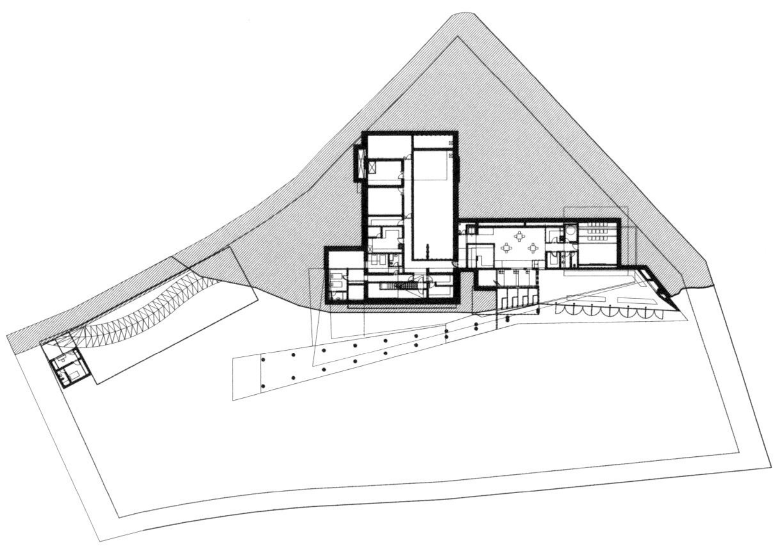

Basement

to his mind, has the power to transform the gaze. How can systems of surprise be recreated within a site when what surrounds it is threatened? How does one merge with chaos without over-expressing it or, on the contrary, denying it? Relating strongly to these questions, structure is approached entirely in its capacity to make architecture. The poured-in-place concrete has been left in its raw state, without veneer, fully expressing the tensions at play. The imposing, 13-metre cantilever hanging over the main living room called for complex balancing strategies. Embedded in the limestone rock, the house is stabilised by a counterweight of equivalent dimensions at the back. The cantilever loads are distributed diagonally by means of a central arm, avoiding the need for any other vertical load-bearing elements. This arm, which, structurally speaking, can be assimilated to a branch, is significantly thinner at its end. Thus, its thickness tapers down from 120 to 30 centimetres, producing a important gradient on the underside. This very tense slope intensifies the inhabitant's relationship to the outside and makes it impossible to clearly assess its proportions. Likewise, by shrinking or expanding the space, it generates shifts in scale inside the house that create unexpected variations. And to counter the deformations of the cantilever, which generates these highly troubling situations of opening between inside and outside, man and the world, the engineer used post-tensioning on the reinforcements after the concrete was poured. As with many YTAA projects, there is a daring—never overplayed—in the implementation of the structures, which are always left visible. And while a very close and exact collaboration was necessary between the architect and the structural engineer, the same goes for the general contractor whose formworkers and

View of the vast living room, almost devoid of vertical bearing elements and level with the natural ground

View during construction of the large concrete cantilevered façade into which the glazing of the retractable façade will be inserted

ironworkers performed their tasks with great precision. Demonstrating genuine craftsmanship, they were responsible in particular for managing the various phases of stripping the formwork and for producing the perfect texture of the concrete, over which a 3-cm-thick, sanded and squared pine cladding was applied. A mixture of black and white cement, the colour of the concrete is also very specific, emitting a soft light while partially absorbing light at the same time.

Karine Dana

Next page: **The large roof staircase opens onto a landscaped walkway. A herb garden and an open-air swimming pool top the villa's accessible roof.**

USJ Innovation, Economy and Sports Campus

Beirut, Lebanon
2004–2012

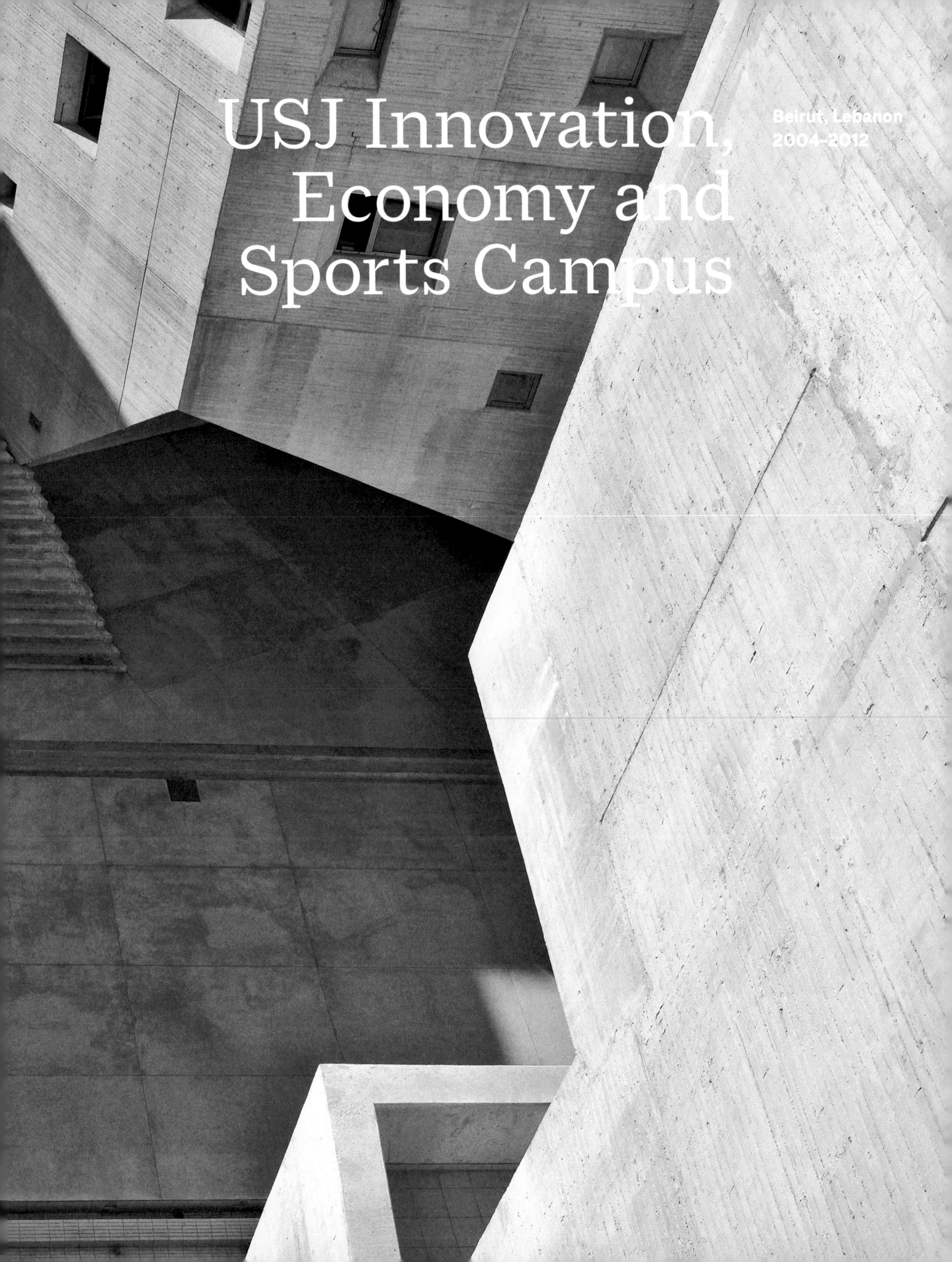

Beirut is a city of many cultures and religious communities that live together in close proximity. Throughout history, it has been a refuge for oppressed religious and ethnic groups and the politically persecuted, and one cannot help but be impressed by the sheer diversity of influences that colour the city. After the conflicts of the past, the hope is that the different denominations can find a new sense of cohesion and that Beirut could once again become a model for the entire region through its collective unity.

Some four kilometres south of the port where in August 2020 the terrible explosion of a depot occurred, causing extensive damage and suffering, lies the campus of the Catholic University of Saint Joseph (USJ) on Rue de Damas. This new building is the most important and by far the largest single building that Youssef Tohme has realised, with 109 Architectes, in his career to date, and it has brought him international acclaim. It is also one of his first works as an architect in Lebanon after completing his studies and gaining professional experience in major architecture offices in France. Tohme's design talent was recognised, and in 2004 he was invited to take on the significant task of co-designing the campus buildings for the Universtiy of Saint Joseph. Work was interrupted as the political situation in Lebanon deteriorated and armed conflict ensued, and Tohme was first able to continue working on the project in 2008 after another spell in France.
They began work on a bold concept that with its unusual internal organisation and idiosyncratic Brutalist expression initially met with scepticism from the client. Eventually They won them over with a strategy of bringing the heterogeneity of the city into the project, extending the public space vertically, and finding a compact solution to the arrangement of the different uses in the lower levels, including four levels of underground parking.
Sixty thousand square metres of usable space are squeezed onto a plot footprint of only 6,000 square metres, which is utilised to the maximum. Situated in a quarter of the city where nothing of the old urban structure remains, the design of the campus conveys a sense of autonomous unity without appearing monolithic. Comprising several separate sections, the complex appears monumental and accessible at the same time, and it is this that constitutes its special fascination. As Tohme remarks, it is the antithesis of a freestanding building.
The programme consists primarily of lecture halls, a large auditorium, administration facilities and a swimming pool and sports hall. The

The expansive southeast elevation is divided into four sections, with the sports hall and swimming pool on the left.

Previous page: **The central public space with its pool and broad flight of stairs**

C
B

incorporation of public space into the building complex reveals the concerns of an architect intent on creating places of public urban interaction in a city that had effectively lost its public places as a result of the civil war. As Tohme says, "the empty space is a direct expression of freedom". He placed a public space in the heart of the complex that in its form resembles an urban interior and through which he organises access to and from the campus. One can look out in different directions onto the surrounding city. This central court flows upwards as a spatial continuum, extending up and along an exterior staircase wide enough for students to sit on. This in turn leads up to the roof terrace that provides spaces for both leisure activities and peace and tranquillity, for example in the rooftop chapel. The importance the the architects attach to this public space produces a highly unusual vertical organisation in which the individual elements of the programme are superimposed over one another. It is as if one had thoroughly shaken up what was once a monolithic block and then pulled it apart to form three parts, each of which is further divided into smaller units and interconnected via footbridges. The different spatial strands cross and connect, compete with one another, or overlap. From this a complex structure emerges.

The first block, to the south, stands out from the others with its façade cladding of lightweight polycarbonate panels. It contains the sports facilities stacked one on top of the other: above an open space on the ground floor is the sports hall, a swimming pool and, on the roof, a basketball court. In the second block, above a large, glazed auditorium and a café on the ground floor, are a music hall and seminar rooms, and at the very top a chapel. On the ground floor of the third block is the main entrance foyer and

One of the main entrances next to the main stairs

Left page: **A multitude of pathways provides views through and into the complex.**

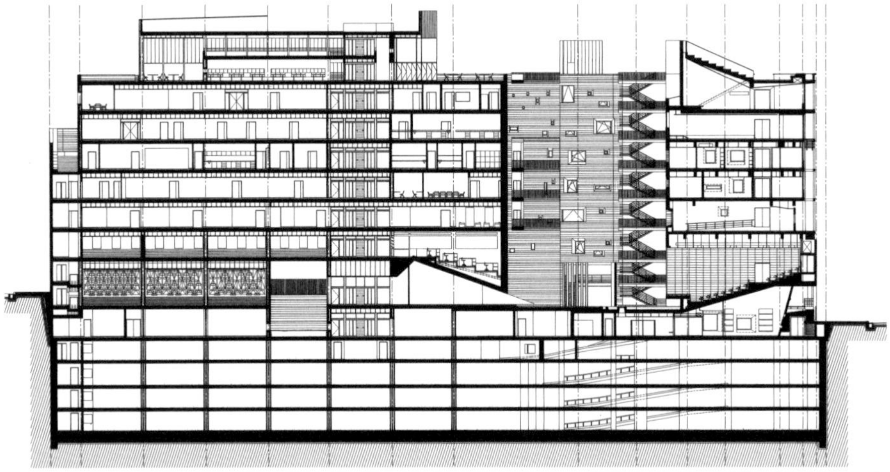

Section through the central courtyard

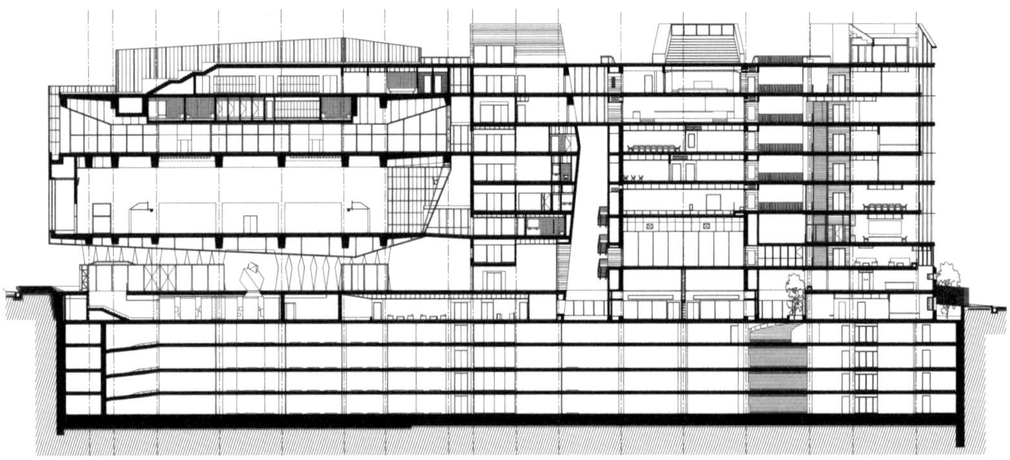

Section through the sports hall and swimming pool

infirmary, and an amphitheatre-like lecture hall. Above these are the library, more seminar rooms and a rooftop restaurant.

This complex organisational structure follows a constructive logic that, with the exception of the grid in the lecture rooms, does not seem to follow a discernible pattern. It is almost as if the functional programme has been inserted into a seemingly endless spatial form that might almost have already existed, and in which the uses have found a home.

Precisely because the in-situ cast concrete exteriors of the separate volumes provide scant indication of what lies behind, one's attention focuses on the flow of interlocking public space. Slit, pierced, and broken open in varying, often playful arrangements of openings, the up to 25 metre high solid concrete walls resist customary interpretation. The dramatic composition of forms tests the limits of formwork and casting techniques, and the result is a testament to the skill and capabilities of the contractors.

The roof can also be used by students for sporting activities.

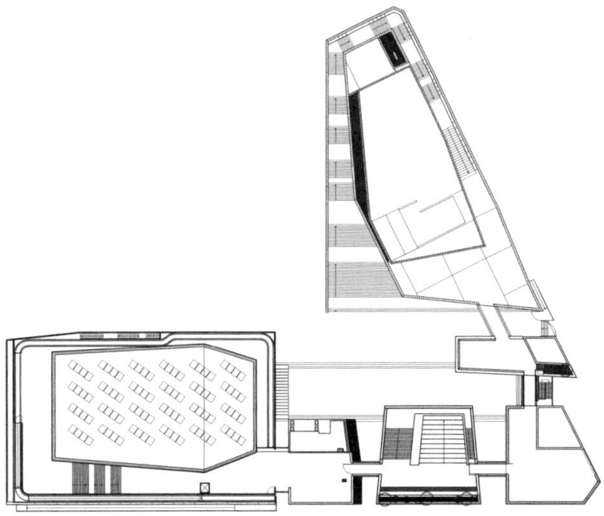

6th floor plan

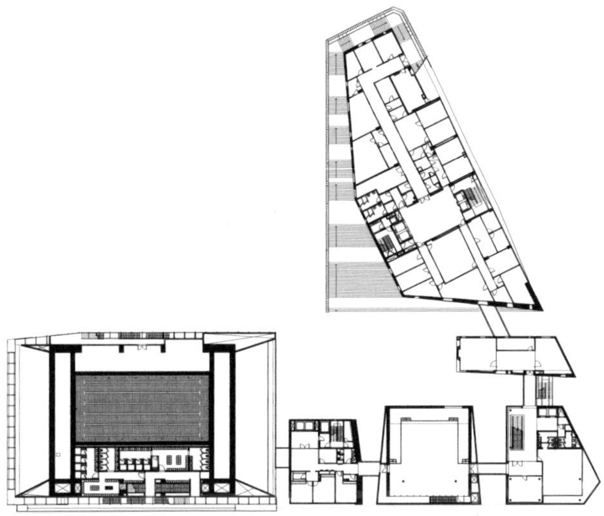

2nd floor plan

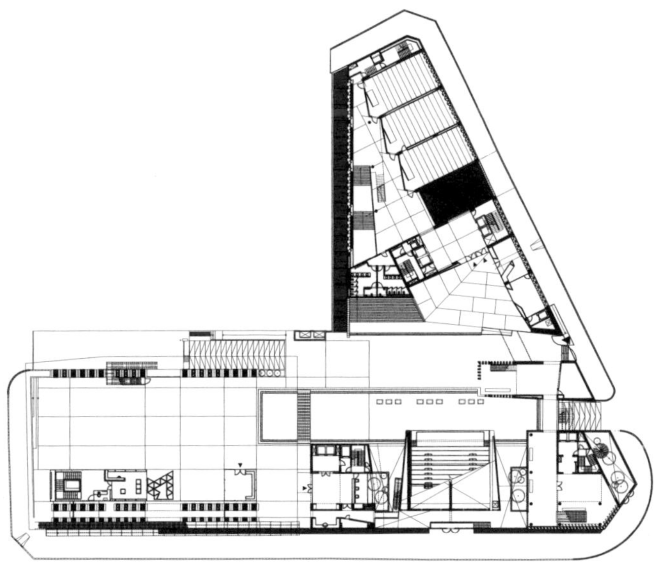

Ground floor plan

Left page: **View through the window of the large lecture hall**

The large lecture hall opens onto the central public space.

View into a foyer with the semi-transparent façade behind

The exposed concrete façades have very different kinds of perforations.

The southeast front of the building is large and striking and divided into four building sections. Here the façades display a distinct language of their own. With the exception of two large "shop windows", the openings are scattered across the façade with an apparent randomness that recalls the impact of missile strikes. While no doubt an intentional gesture, it comes close to aestheticising the horrors of war, but the overall effect is certainly visually compelling.
The colour of the exposed concrete is not consistent throughout, tending towards pink in some places. As Tohme explains, the quarry supplying the white sand ceased operations during the construction and the sand subsequently imported from Cyprus had a significantly more reddish pigment. This reflects the constant unpredictability that is an economic reality in Lebanon. As such, this university building is highly symbolic of its surrounding context at multiple levels.

Sebastian Redecke

Ilot sur le Parc

Marseille, France
2019–ongoing

Pushing back against prevailing policies in property development, which tend to do away with existing fabrics by introducing exogenous programming under the pretext of improving neighbourhoods, the office of Youssef Tohme Architects & Associates approached this operation by considering the preservation of social heritage as a force for projects, activities and landscape.

Landscaped mass plan of the block envisioned as a social structure, a fragment of city dedicated to activities and residents

Located in a working-class district near the St-Charles train station and the point where the motorway enters the city, the Ilot sur le Parc is the last mixed-development zone (ZAC) of the Euroméditerranée 1 project, overseen by the public urban development agency of the same name. The YTTA office's proposal for this operation is conceived as a critical response to lack of any real consideration for Marseille's residential fabric and the plurality of its social classes in the approach adopted by Euroméditerranée 1, which has essentially contributed to enhancing the historical, entrepreneurial and tourist qualities of the city of Marseille.

With its triangular geometry, the block formed by the Ilot sur le Parc is west-facing on one side, where it is composed of old buildings in a north-south alignment, overlooks a new public park on a second side, and is south-facing on its third side, which overlooks the nineteenth-century Triumphal Arch at the Porte d'Aix. Refusing to indulge in any glorification of built heritage—an attitude that all too often hides the real urban problems—the architects do not seek to respond to this symbolic arch with another façade, but develop their project strategy from a void.

Thus, they avail of the situation of the Triumphal Arch, which they face by imagining another doorway, a gap open to the city and the wider landscape, composed of a transparent mesh, whose framework becomes looser on the higher floors. This mesh will be extended by a large monumental staircase at the entrance to the block, offering several heights for perspectives on the city as well as connections to it.

"While all the actors in the project were pushing us to respond to the prerogatives of the Architecte des Bâtiments de France, who was in favour of a 'built' architectural response for the design of this southern façade, we defended the importance of constructing a void, a continuity rather than a solid form. This resistance, which we maintained to the end, represented the key entry point for us towards a completely different approach to the orientation of this district and its programming. By opening up the block to use, to all forms of relationships, to local people, to proximity and to the wider landscape, we wanted to support a social idea of the city, closely linked to the existing forces already in place", explains Youssef Tohme.

This decisive approach relates to initiatives that have already been undertaken locally, conducive to a better appropriation of public spaces and the emergence of an engaged urbanism open to the dynamics already operating in neighbouring districts. It stems from a highly attentive examination of the existing situation, understood in all its thickness and all its layers, not only in terms of buildings but also, and above all, in terms of people and residents. Thus, the urban fabric is approached in all its complexity, its potential for hybridisation, its difficulties and its strong points, which must be extended, improved and interconnected.

In response to this absolute necessity to generate the project from the uses, exchanges and needs of the population, the office developed a distinct approach to the block, envisaged as a social structure, a fragment of the city linked to activities and residents. Thus, going against any idea of a generic and standardised product, the

In their design for the façade overlooking the emblematic Triumphal Arch at the Porte d'Aix, the architects wished to build a void rather than a solid form.

architects deploy a multiple, interrelated and yet unitary vision of the block within the city. Taking on several faces according to the typological relationships it stands in relation to—the new public park, the Place Jules Guesde, its inner core, the wider landscape, the working-class context—this block is not considered as an architectural object, a totality closed by its facades, but as an open, living and evolving topographic device.

Its mixed programming, which favours integration initiatives for the benefit of underprivileged inhabitants of Marseille, has been designed and adapted according to the practices of this block, which is meant to be explored, appropriated and shared. Thus, a "tiers-lieu"—the programme's unifying activity—is placed deep within the plot, in its heart, requiring people to walk through it. The existing buildings—rehabilitated as little as possible while preserving the variations in floor

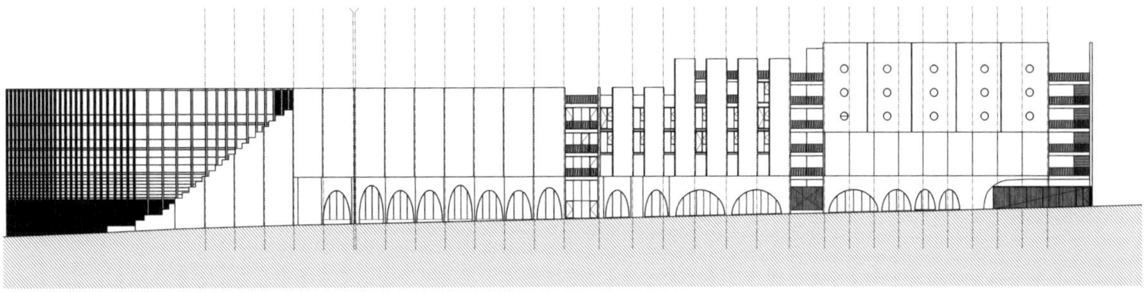

East façade

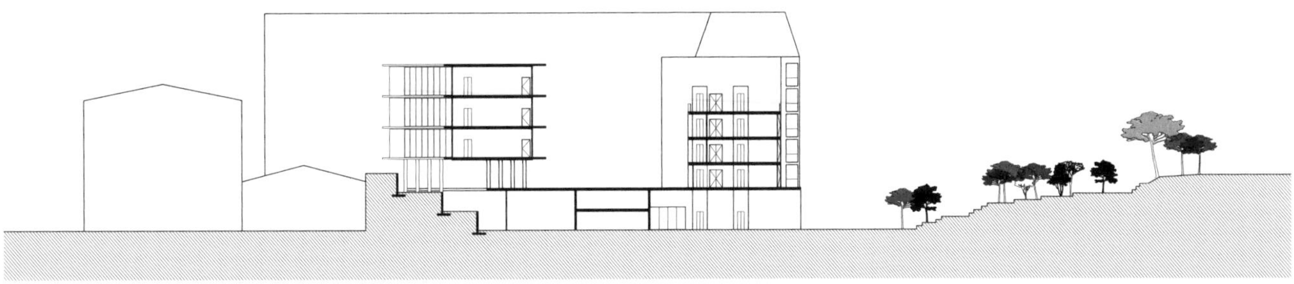

Cross-section

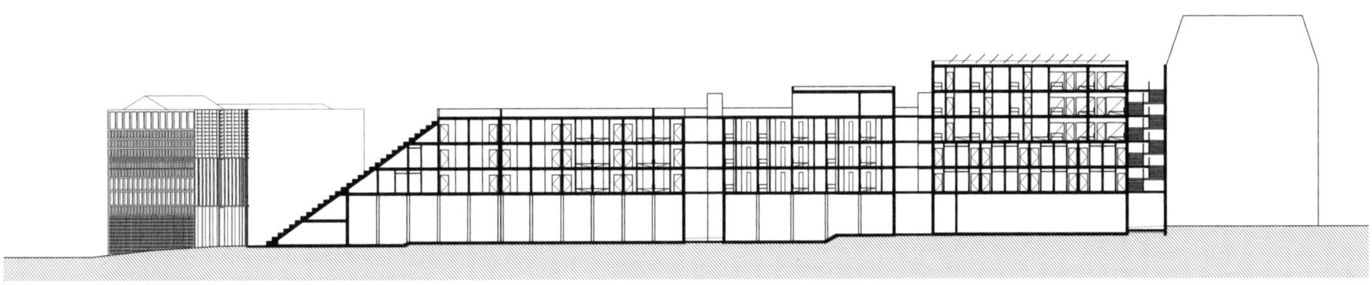

Longitudinal section

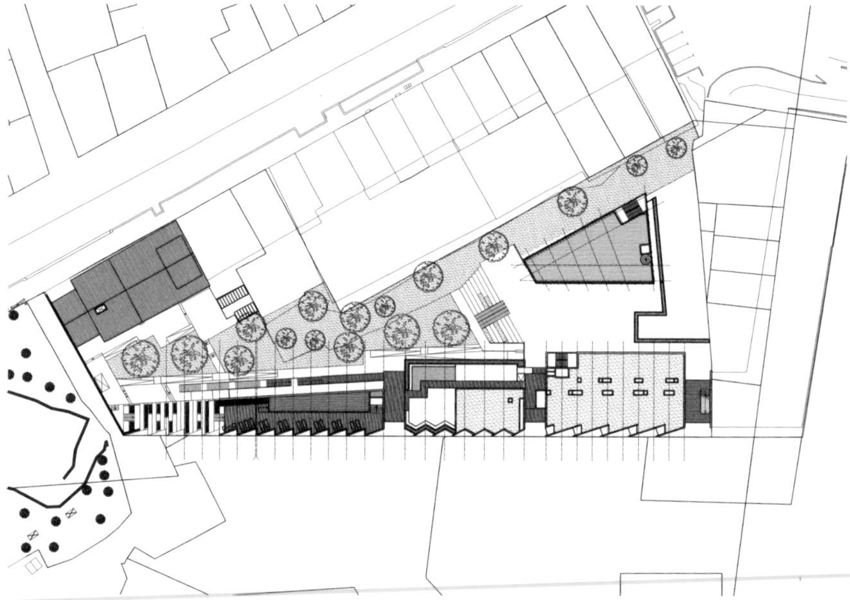

Roof plan

4th floor plan

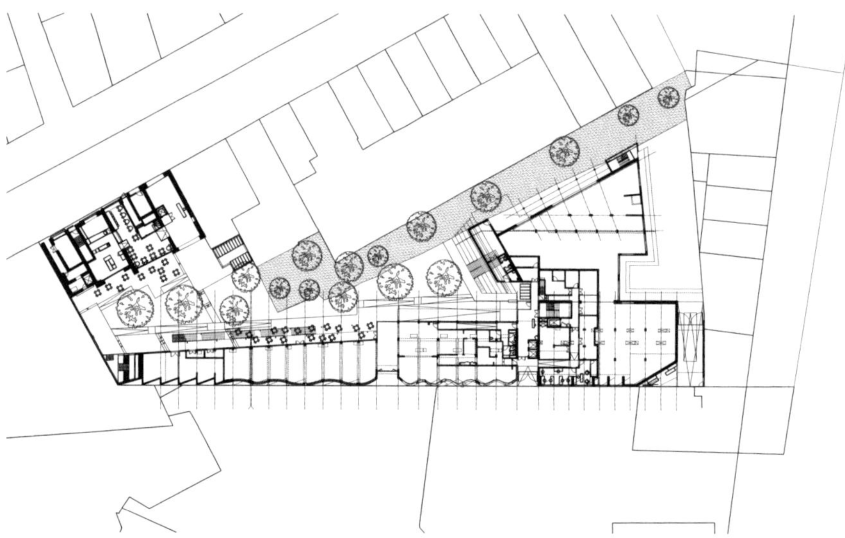

Ground floor plan

Photomontage showing the porosity of the mesh façade, allowing the new programmes to filter into the heart of the site

heights and their spatial specificities—contain co-living spaces. Roof terraces accessible to the public create new, open spaces with a view of Notre-Dame de la Garde, the hills of Provence and the wider landscape. Local activities and services will be housed on the ground floors of the rehabilitated buildings, while restaurant spaces will be inserted in the heart of the planted block. Finally, affordable hotel accommodation, characterised by typological variety, will take up the three new buildings along the park.

Through this highly specific programmatic and spatial response, the architects propose a reflection on the importance of legitimising and facilitating what happens between people and spaces, because this is above all how the city is produced and renewed.

Karine Dana

A599 Apartment Building

Ashrafieh, Beirut, Lebanon
2013–2019

This project is emblematic of the way in which Youssef Tohme Architects & Associates explores the disruptive and conductive power of a structure to create a habitat, to connect and to produce calm and pleasure in the heart of a very noisy and fragmented inner-city urban fabric.

In the busy Ashrafieh district of Beirut, an important area of Christian resistance with one of the highest population densities in the city, a corner plot with a triangular geometry presents a 10-metre difference in grade from north to south. The context: a high level of street noise, high-rise buildings that have replaced traditional buildings, a school and a shopping centre with a public space on the roof; strong shifts in scale, noise barriers, but also a clear view to the sea. The project taps into this imaginary of openness while engaging with an array of topographical, sonic and visual inconsistencies and asperities—causing discomfort but also producing an intensity specific to Beirut. It demonstrates how a rather disruptive environment can become the basis for rethinking the project. Accepted as they are, in all their singularity and reality, the existing constraints in fact enable a reversal of the architectural approach.

Taking his cue from these conditions of instability, which necessarily call for strategies of adaptation and invention, the architect presented the client with the idea of designing an apartment building whose plans could be adapted freely to the residents' inclinations, uses and needs. The planning permission request was consequently submitted on the basis of a "capable" construction, suited to absorbing modifications. The design proposal was more about a structure that quite generously defines contours, heights, projections, recesses and openings than about housing per se. "This project is an experiment that the developer was willing to go along with. We did not want to pre-determine any way of living, which, in such a complex context, would have been a mistake. Our project structure thus responds to unforeseeable urban and domestic contingencies", explains the architect.

Each of the 450-square-metre floor plates can be divided freely, both horizontally and vertically, offering multiple and specific ways of living, all provided by the structure. Featuring large open surfaces with a ceiling height of 3.60 metres, in-ground gardens enclosed in terraces to the south to provide a filter to the city, open-air

Right page: **The apartment building is located in the Ashrafieh district of Beirut, an emblematic sector of Christian resistance and one of the most densely populated areas in the city.**

GlobeMed
N 160488

In situ view of the building and the uneven, high-rise urban background

rooms to the north, such as the alcoves on 4-metre cantilevers, and large immersive openings to the fore, the structure offers three levels of relationship with the city: protection, intimacy and proximity. Approached from the inside, it combines urban situations with ways of inhabiting that relate to just as many lifestyles, whether open, closed, superimposed or decompartmentalised, in continuity with the outside, and independently of the interior decoration. Here, living is akin to the vital layer of architecture. The affinity between structure and lifestyle is particularly perceptible in this project, in which the architect does not intervene in the "interior" spaces. The latter can be freely appropriated by the resident, who thus constructs his or her own relationship with the city and the exterior. However, the fundamental conditions for living are present: light, air, space and open ground. In this context of freedom of occupation and structural capacity, vegetation easily finds its place and reinforces this idea of focusing on the essential. By designing this structure for an urban habitat like the first part of an urban block that very rigorously complies with regulations, densities of scale and proximity, alignments and projections,

Detail of the cantilevered interior cavities overlooking the street

the architect seeks to initiate a way of thinking about the city and a generative process that opens up to the possibility of collective living without neglecting individual needs.
How can architecture be structuring in such an exuberant urban context? How can we return, through habitat, to the importance of an urban structure that frames, calms and clarifies a situation of such density and clutter? The structure, which is highly defined and forms an open monolith through the sole use of concrete, with all windows and doors set back, is akin to an inhabited monument, in the continuity of the urban

Next page: **Each 450-square-metre floor plate is freely divisible, horizontally or vertically, offering multiple and specific modes of inhabitation.**

Forming an open concrete monolith, the structure resembles an inhabited monument.

Right page: In situ view of the building and the highly urbanised Lebanese mountains in the background

South façade

North façade

fabric, aligned to the north and projecting more freely to the south. Its bevelled angle gives it the necessary width to open up to the city and let light from the east into the dwellings, which thus have triple exposure. The programming of this capable building is also defined as is it progressively inhabited. A gym and an open-air swimming pool were later integrated into a remaining part of the living areas.
Here again, the structural design is what defines the architecture. Consisting of a core and load-bearing façades made of cast concrete, the structure determines the façades, positioned in relation to the regularity of the pillars. The challenge for the engineer was to make his calculations according to the layout of the openings desired by the architect and the thinness of the slab. The engineer used post-tensioning systems, so that the slab is not deformed. The colour the architect selected to tint the concrete, which required dark sands, and the use of the same gravel, cements and colouring agents for the whole project added further constraints and had the effect of lowering the overall strength of the structure. To address this issue, silica fume was combined with the colouring agents during the mixing process to significantly reinforce the building.

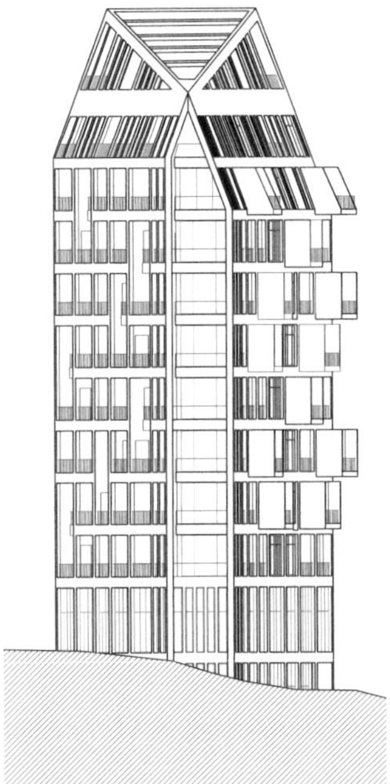

East façade

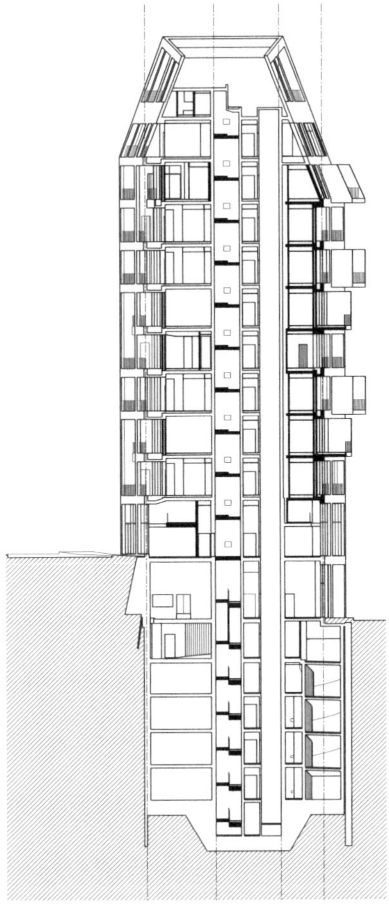

Cross-section

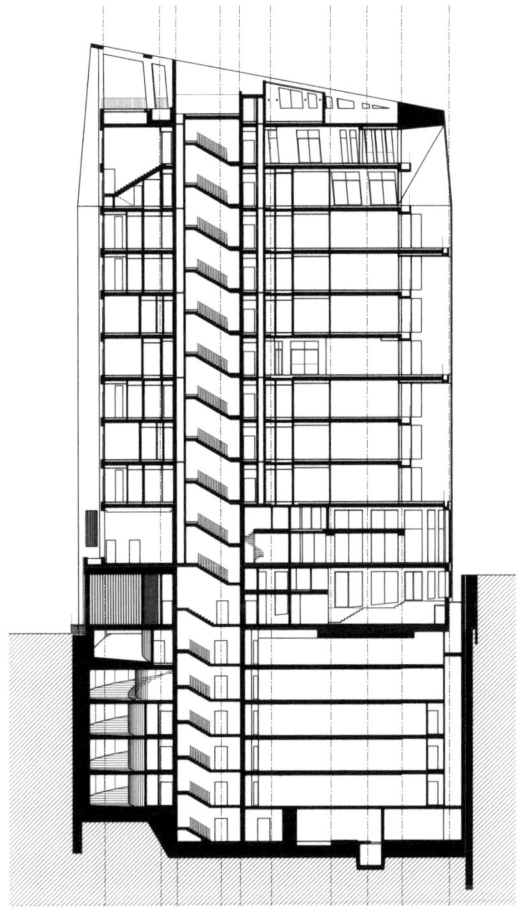

Longitudinal section

Undertaking a project of this kind in the middle of the city, involving the pouring of large surfaces of concrete on the same day to avoid joints, was also a challenge, as was the design of the formwork, which had to be adapted to this irregular geometry and required very rigorous strategies for surface continuity. The resulting sharpness of this angular concrete structure, again approached in an artisanal manner, gives the building its strength in the city, inviting the passer-by to perceive its precision, and the care with which it was built, qualities that are so often lacking in current constructions.

Karine Dana

View of a housing terrace and a floor plate that can be freely appropriated

Right page: View of the façade facing the sea with its cantilevered "rooms" overlooking the city

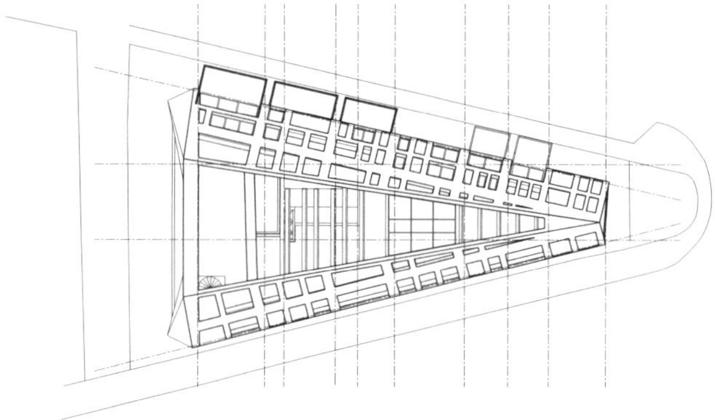

Roof plan

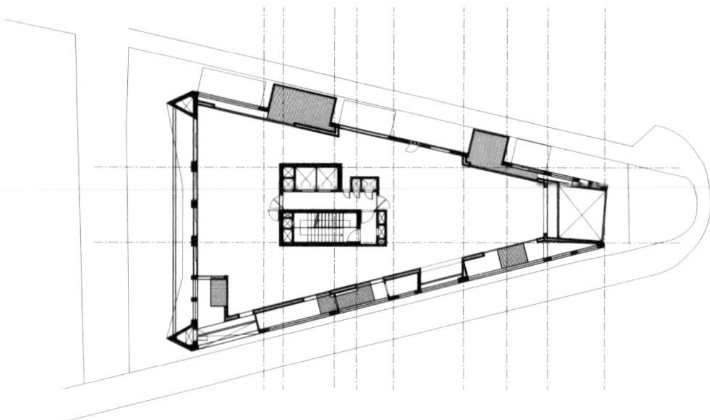

Typical floor showing the structure and the circulation core

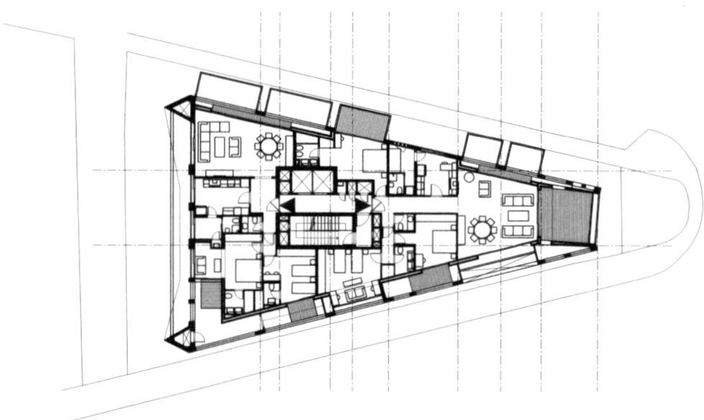

Floor with two apartments

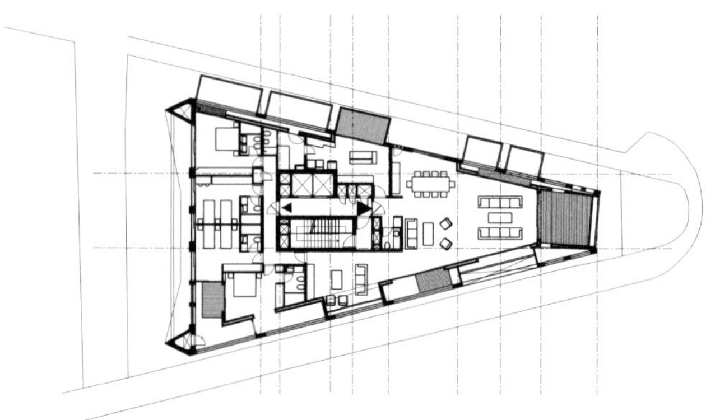

Floor with one apartment

To the fore of the building, a bevelled angle provides the width necessary to open up to the city and let light from the east enter the apartments, which thus benefit from a triple exposure.

MARe
MARe

MARe—Muzeul de Artă Recentă

Bucharest, Romania
2013-2018

The Muzeul de Artă Recentă (MARe, Museum of Recent Art) is a private museum and gallery in Bucharest which opened in 2018. For the site on a street corner in the wealthy Primăverii (Spring) residential district, Youssef Tohme Architects & Associates devised a unique architectural concept that has its origins in the building that formerly occupied the site.

The residential villa, built in 1939, was confiscated by the communists in 1948. Ana Pauker, a committed Stalinist who actively supported the purging and deportation of political opponents, took up residence in the villa. Rising quickly through the ranks, she became foreign minister and deputy prime minister of the new regime in Romania. Only a few years later, however, she fell from grace and was forced to withdraw from the political elite. For years, the villa of the much-despised politician stood empty, a grim and eerie sight behind tall trees, despite lying just 200 metres from Nikolae and Elena Ceaușescu's sumptuous residence, now also a museum.

The villa was purchased by a Lebanese businessman, Roger El Akoury, who experienced the civil war in his homeland in the early 1990s and moved to Bucharest where he founded a successful business and developed a passion for Romanian modern art from the 1960s to the present day. His collection now encompasses some 600 works of art from different genres of painting, sculpture, installation, photography, collage, and concept and video art, and also includes works by many comparatively unknown artists. Together they provide a comprehensive overview of art from the period of communist dictatorship as well as after the 1989 revolution right up to present-day artistic movements.

El Akoury acquired the house to display works from his collection as well as temporary exhibitions with loans from abroad. In addition, he wanted to create an open meeting place for the city's cultural scene.

While it was clear to the client that the old building had to be demolished, he also wanted a new building to take into account the history of the site with its old villa. He turned to Youssef Tohme to develop a concept, who came up with a bold proposal: to demolish the unloved old building as discussed but also to rebuild it anew as an opaque shell with bricked-in windows and moreover to elevate the entire structure off the ground above a glazed ground floor. What makes the idea so compelling is that it allows the house and its dark political past to remain symbolically present but also reveals the contrasting modern

The museum appears to float above a glazed ground floor.

Romania within, with its lively and diverse art scene. For El Akoury as well as for the architect Tohme, the design also recalls the lack of freedom and the persecution they experienced in younger years back home in Lebanon, and this probably gave them added impetus to push ahead with the idea. Without their experiences, it is unlikely they would have arrived at such a powerful and concise idea.

The new building has five levels, a large roof terrace with beautiful views of the city and a small outdoor space in the courtyard at the back that, like the terrace, can be used for events such as exhibition openings or book presentations. From outside, the museum does indeed appear to float as envisaged by the architect, the five-metre-high glazed ground level lending the building an inviting sense of lightness and openness that contrasts with the heavy building mass above. Huge, sliding floor-to-ceiling glass panels open onto the courtyard. While the main entrance, reception area and bookstore face onto the street corner, the extensive rearward section is used for catering.

The monolithic block housing the upper levels has a striking presence, its outer form echoing that of the former villa as a hard-to-fathom ghost of a dark past. Instead of casting the new

The bricked-in openings recall the ghost of the former villa that once stood on the site.

Left page: **The sheltered courtyard and café at the rear**

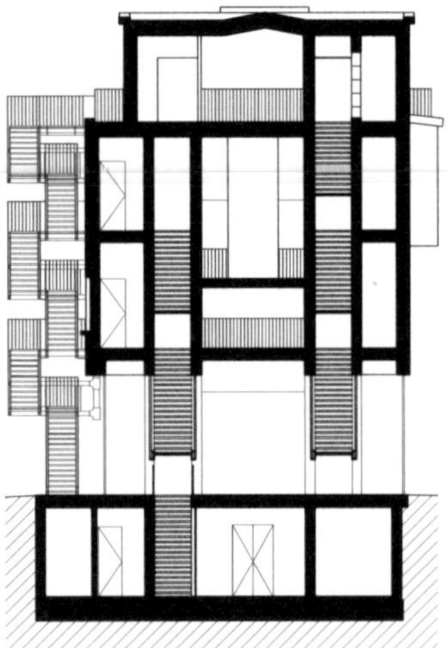

Cross-section

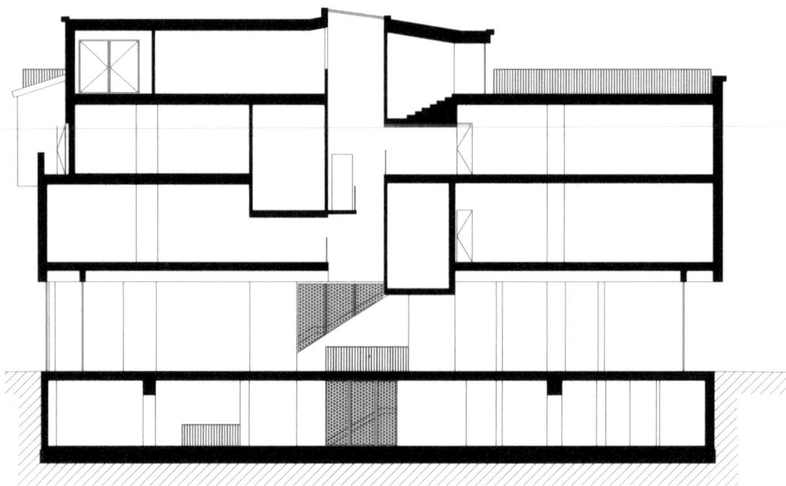

Longitudinal section

old villa in exposed concrete, as was originally planned, the architects have rendered the entire building in small-format black bricks that bring out the idea of the abstract shell even more strongly. The windows, arches and roof cornices are all clearly visible, turning the building into a dramatic, large-scale sculpture.

A central atrium spanning the top four levels allows light in from above and gives visitors the opportunity to grasp the building in its entirety. Two single flights of stairs flank the atrium.

In contrast to the pervasive openness of the entrance area, Tohme took a different approach for the upper floors and the basement. The stairs of the atrium lead to convoluted, windowless gallery spaces and corridors that in their arrangement consciously subvert one's expectations of a clearly organised museum. Instead of white, neutral boxes, the building is a labyrinth of small rooms and narrow corridors that aim to create and heighten a sense of intimacy between the visitors and the artworks. The confined circulation spaces and modest atrium, painted black, create a distinct contrast to the

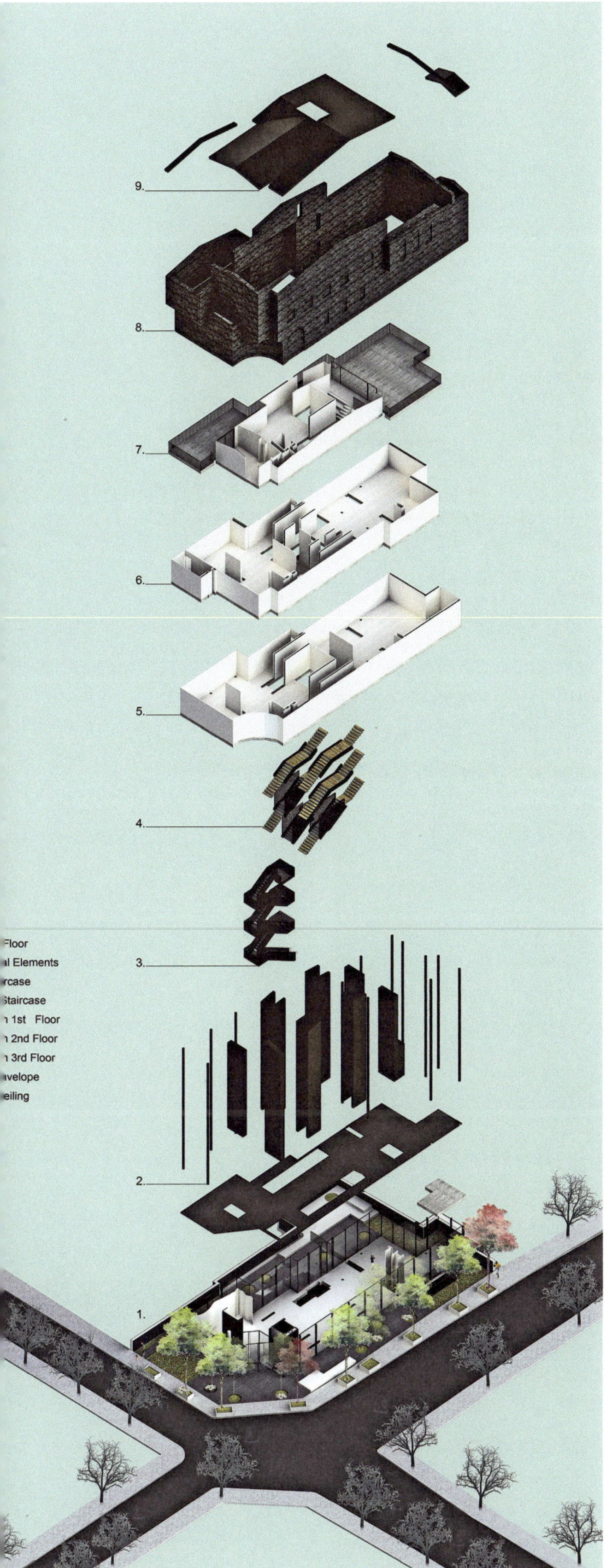

Exploded drawing of the individual elements of the new building

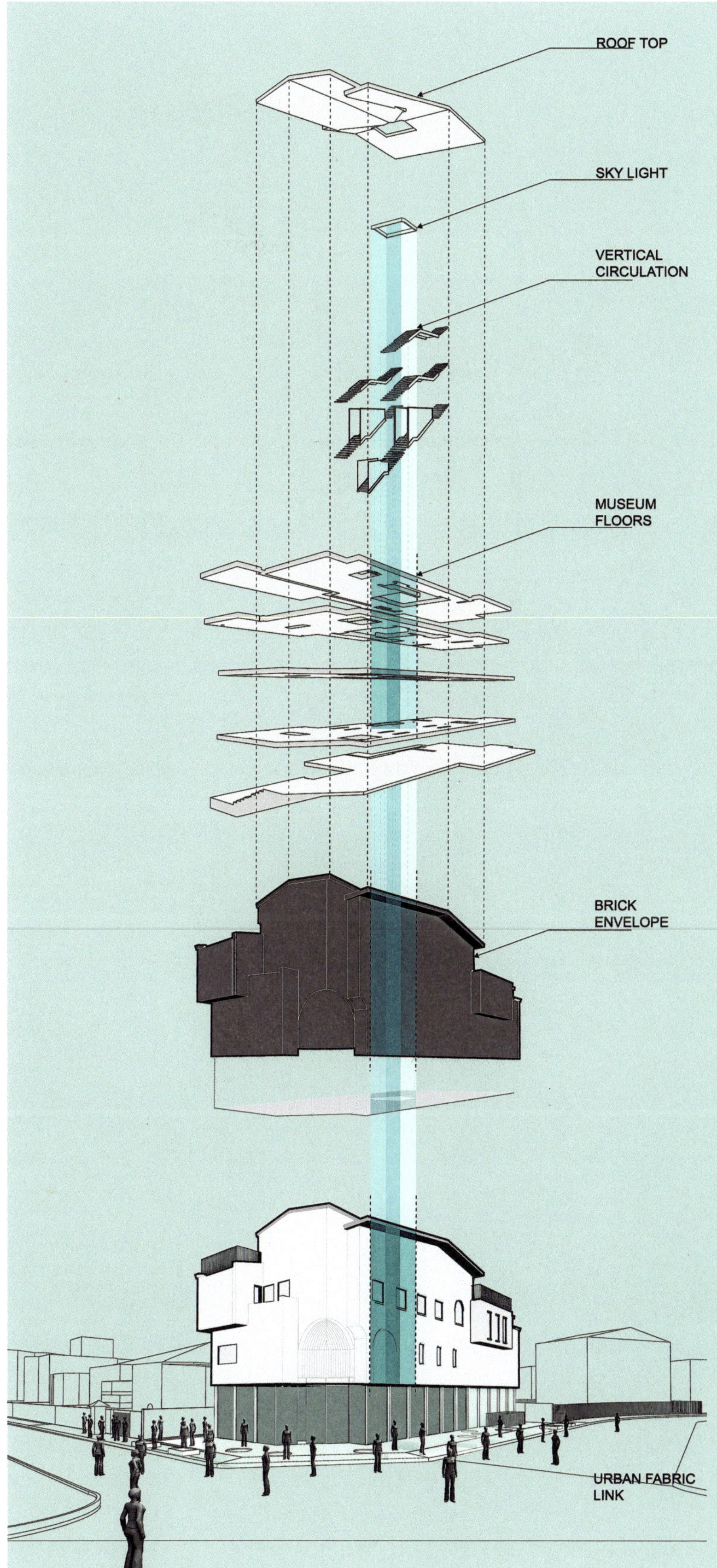

Conceptual drawing of the building structure and its brick envelope

Main entrance with the concave curved brick wall

View back to the main entrance

The twin staircases in the middle of the building

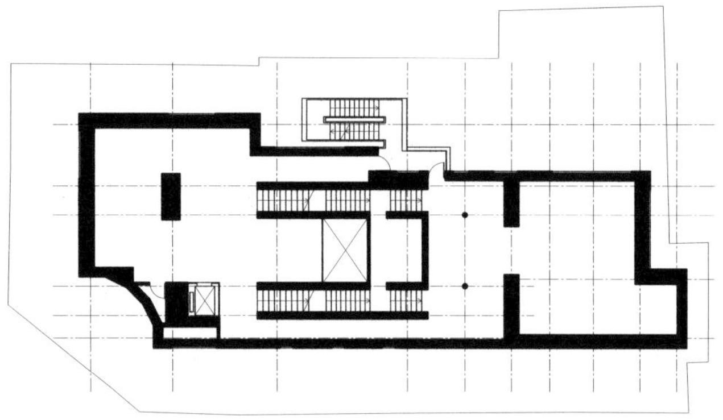

3rd floor plan

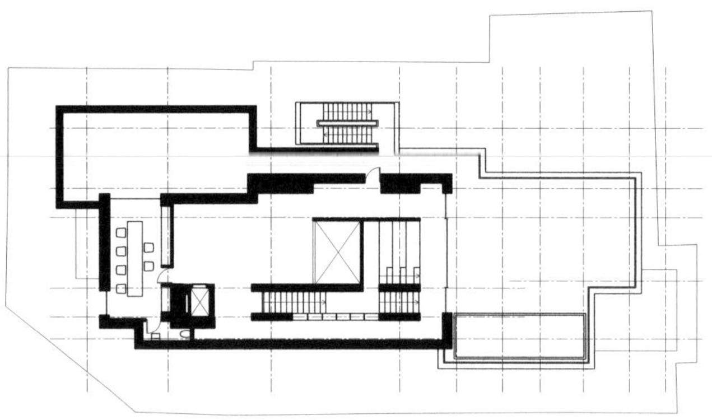

1st floor plan

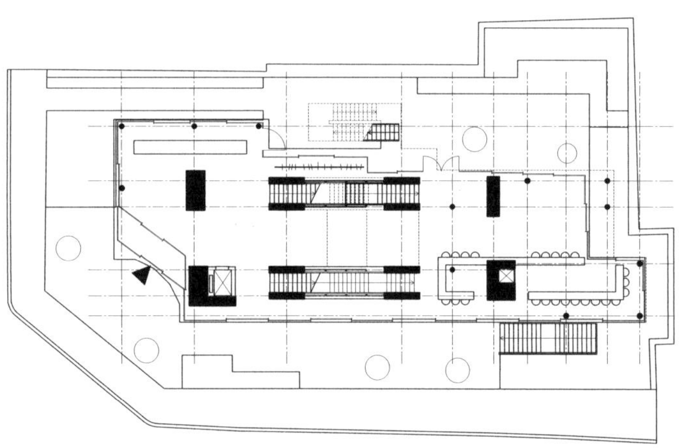

Ground floor plan

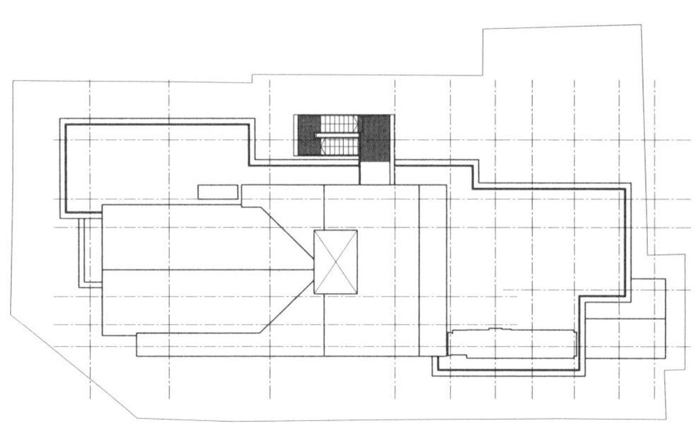

Mass plan

Right page: **The confines of the site and the rediscovered bunker in the former cellar made construction conditions difficult.**

A small exhibition space between the stairs

art spaces. Niches adjoining the atrium can be used as small intermediate levels for temporary exhibitions. There is method to this unusual arrangement: Tohme's constrained interiors aim to immerse visitors in a world reminiscent of that of the former dictatorial regime: confining, prescriptive and opaque. At times this also constrains the presentation of some of the exhibits. On the top floor, a small forum space with stepped seating was added as a library space.

During demolition, a bunker for the former occupant was discovered in the basement. This has been retained and repurposed as an auditorium with state-of-the-art audio and video technology. Of all Youssef Tohme's works to date, the MARe is perhaps his boldest and clearest articulation of a conceptual intention and, alongside its narrative qualities, is most expressive of its historical and political dimensions.

Sebastian Redecke

Sectional view of all five levels of the new building

Next page: Visitors can grasp the building as a whole from the central atrium.

An exhibition space on the 1st floor

Conversation between Youssef Tohme and Karine Dana

I would like us to have a conversation together that continues to transform… The starting point is the most important thing, because the discussion will not really end.
Can you tell us how a project starts?

As an architect, I'm looking for a relationship to the world that is both very precise and undefined: the sensation of being within a place, like in the desert, in the sea, or above the clouds. Three hundred sixty degrees of emptiness charged with space. This fundamental quest is common to all our projects.
I constantly aspire to construct a state free of references, a state in which the self is simultaneously grounded and suspended and to which one can merely belong. It is a condition of absolute solitude and, at the same time, of attachment and of a deep bond with the milieu.
I view these situations of indeterminacy and unpredictability, of the absence of limits, as a necessity for human release. Only then can we move through space and have space move through us, and perhaps, be purged of our anxieties. This very strong connection, this feeling of being here, at the same time as the world, in its present, in its thickness, in its mass and its movement is a preliminary to everything I want to design and build. I want to create places where there are no bearings, that induce dizziness and silence: places in "aeroplane mode"!
Consequently, for each of the office's projects, we always set out to create a dynamic and its opposite. It's a way of having

the human subject enter a state of release, like an extraordinarily physical and present state. I seek this state of porosity in mankind, of awakening and intoxication by space, the kind of state that love or a kiss can plunge us into. All our architecture stems from the quest for this relationship: the immensely fragile moment of contact between the intimate and the collective. The collective is not about number, the collective is the milieu. This obsessive search is a determining factor in my work. It explains all my temptations. It is a search for naivety. A dreamlike state, a state of open freedom that I would like to touch through each of my projects.

What spatial experiences left a lasting impression on you?

My childhood was steeped in fundamental spatial experiences. That of sea, above all: the only landscape you can really enter. Being in the sea, touching its softness, being surrounded by the effects of the wind on the water, being part of it. This situation provides incredible strength while stripping away all sense of orientation. The feeling of being connected to something bigger than oneself and at the same time being within this space is so special… This is due in particular to the lack of any possible projection and representation. I find this very affecting.
The sea taught me the meaning of atmosphere and sensation. When I want to immerse myself in an architecture and understand it, I frown and squint at it, as if I were underwater, without a mask, but with my eyes open all the same. It was by opening my eyes that I learned what the sea was. It's not just a question of seeing it but of entering it. Letting your skin and your pupils at the same time feel and experience the contact. It's a very physical feeling but also a

feeling of total escape. Maybe that's the definition of an atmosphere in fact. The sea taught me about architecture. It teaches us that even when everything is blocked, you can still escape.

When I began my architectural studies, I analysed port or maritime cities. Why does one feel so good in these cities? I understood that in a city, the mere presence of the sea fosters social bonds and detaches us from everything.

The sea has the power to take over the built environment, public space, roads, words and noise. The sea teaches us silence and abstraction. I also understood that the sea could erase the limits of any established order, of any power in place. You call out to it, it comes to you and it fills you, spreading out even if you only have a small space. The sea produces effacement and escape because it shifts us off centre. It is very important today that we remind ourselves that the human being is no longer the centre.

The sea has had an enormous impact on me and on the way I work, from the smallest to the largest spaces, whether private or public. I have the same perception in the desert or on a rooftop, of inhabiting a power. That's where it all starts: creating penetrable landscapes in which people live, walk down, float, swim, talk, keep quiet.

These memories of space never leave me and guide each project. For example, I always try to bring the programme, the use and the structure back to this precise idea of the expanse that invites, assimilates and allows itself to be inhabited. This means that I don't want to define anything but to open up and liberate spaces. I never work on parameters that reduce or invoke reference scales or standards. In this way, a house is never really a house. It is a setting that puts you in your place. And that means losing your bearings. This is fundamental. The greatest spatial experiences that we can have occur when there are absolutely no bearings, when you are empty yourself, emptied, totally available to interact with your milieu. On an equal footing.

I also remember travelling through landscapes by boat where mountainsides came tumbling into the sea. It was very disturbing. I associated mountains with the idea of "layers", succession, sequences. So, the further I progressed on the water, the more the landscape seemed to recede. Every time you got closer to a layer, another one appeared.

In architecture, constructing space from "layers" disrupts reality. It draws us into a dream state. Again, it strips away all bearings to leave a state of total abstraction that simply plays with space.

When our office designed Villa T and Villa SC, the first houses we built in Lebanon, it was precisely the search for these conditions that guided the projects.

We didn't set out to design but to erase. We did not try to represent or to reassure but to blur. We did not try to close or define but to open up and subtract the façades. The Villa SC is a simple low wall with a perforation. The idea of the house disappears in both projects.

In a country where the idea of representation is so strong and so political, how do you position yourself as an architect?

Deciding not to express a representation or an affiliation when you live in Lebanon already amounts to a political stance. I work in a country where identities are numerous and fragmented and where these questions are so entrenched and linked to war… The experience of these fractures, these limits, these conventions and identity

politics is still very vivid for me. As an architect, I fight against these ideas with the weapons of the architect. I have pondered the concepts of representation, which are so prevalent and important in Lebanon, for a long time. This question cannot be easily dismissed because it underlies all action. It therefore has an impact on the territory. This is why I fight to break the weight of image. Because this weight limits, confines, categorises and assimilates. I therefore always try to remove references and I do not wish to represent an illusion of departure. I am only interested in situations of exchange. I seek to build a common bond. As an architect, I believe deeply in gentleness. I think that situations are not always conflicts. I defend a romantic vision of the world. This means that I am idealistic and resilient. I believe there can be delicateness everywhere. The city of Beirut cannot be reduced to an aggressive morphology. There is also a lot of gentleness in the city. A climate, a geography, easy human contact, intensity and warmth. I try to internalise these intimate conditions in my projects. This gentleness induces a specific atmosphere. This is what connects us to Beirut, a certain magic. A resilience that makes it possible to push back all limits. That is what we must keep.

How is this concept of gentleness approached in your projects?

In each of our projects, we try to construct this ambivalent interiority that combines grounding and detachment. As I see it, this is the very definition of the Lebanese condition: a state of permanent contradiction, both tense and placid. I don't want to have anything to do with chaos. I don't want

to use it. I advocate the concept of gentleness in architecture. I consider this as a political stance. Gentleness always comes at the same time and as a reaction to a certain brutality.
When I insert a project into a territory, I always try to calm the situation through architecture, through material, atmosphere and siting. In the situation of extreme confusion in which we currently find ourselves, gentleness is a strong response. It doesn't act as an image or a reference, but as a silence, a mist, a gust of air, like the sea. I am interested in this opposition. I think it produces a real intensity.
Things are tough but we can look at them differently. I refuse the idea of there being an exclusive and unique way of looking. Even when a situation is difficult, you can always bring something new to it.
There is a real power to gentleness as a refusal of aggressiveness and determinism. Being in a state of gentleness makes it easier to listen to the territory. I consider this to be a necessity.
Through our projects, we always try to bring a soothing gaze, which emanates from our attentiveness and alertness.
Gentleness comes through observation. When the sun catches the concrete and enters a space, suddenly the possibility of gentleness arises.
To be gentle is to be understanding. It is also an admission of our vulnerability. It is a choice, a position. There are sensual and spiritual qualities to gentleness. There is a tactile quality linked to touch, to the mouth, to the skin. There is always the possibility of proximity to the abyss too, to brutality and opacity. Any situation that the architect has to face is fraught with worry. Being gentle induces a willingness to understand, to get closer, to trust, to stabilise. It isn't a weakness but a strength. It is a matter of tact and non-resignation. Working with gentleness and practising it means developing an aware-

ness of complexity and probably also maintaining a bond with childhood.

Gentleness is a philosophy of the gaze, a philosophy of presence. It gives you the keys to a phenomenology of space. As an architect, I relate this to a non-materialist approach to space which deals with light, air, silence, void and the reflections of sunbeams.

The concept of gentleness lets us talk about architecture with immaterial means. It's very powerful. It raises the question of the fundamental and primitive nature of a context.

The concept of gentleness expresses a refusal to speak, a resistance against the state of the world, against that language. It is a weapon for an architect in Lebanon or elsewhere to fight against finitude, against all forms of closure, and against certainties.

Gentleness raises the idea of open interiority. This is the opposite of a bubble. As an architect, I don't try to make worlds, but constantly ask myself how to let the outside world in, how far I should open up to it, and how I can bring about exchange. Indeed, gentleness keeps us in the world. We respond to the world. We maintain this porosity.

That's essential.

I do not wish to create situations of isolation through projects, nor temporary illusions of resolution. I bring gentleness into Villa T because the context questions me. I respond by opening myself up as much as possible to the point of making the very image of the house fade away.

Gentleness, as you envision it, seems to embody a new form of radicality… It corresponds both to a point of view and a new beginning…

Yes, it is a form of radicality, just like nuance and blurring. Radicality in architecture, long based on the idea of rupture, is looking for other forms of expression today. For a long time in architecture there was a belief in a radicality of force, war, brusqueness or brilliance. People were frequently pitted against each other in the name of this radicality based on division. It is time to explore other, more subtle paths, paths that are more "in the clouds". While gentleness can be adopted as a stance in architecture, it is expressed upstream of the projects. It is a subtle way of negotiating, of encouraging exchange and of excluding conflict. If there is no longer any power struggle, the situation becomes interesting and favourable to architects. The concept of gentleness in architecture is ultimately very destabilising…

In Lebanon, where there is very little room for silence, where every void must be filled, promoting this vision of gentleness is particularly important. It is a political act. It is a way to silence not only voices and machines, but also signs, connotations and representations. In this respect, gentleness is a good companion to abstraction as well as a precious tool for a project.

In our work on redesigning the Brazza site in Bordeaux, we developed the idea of silence in the public space. Nietzsche's silent "places for reflection" inspired us to create landscape strips that run through this former industrial site from north to south. "One day, and probably soon, we will need some recognition of what is missing primarily in our big cities: quiet and wide, expansive places for reflection—places with long, high ceilinged arcades for bad or all-too-sunny

weather, where no shouts or noise from carriages can penetrate and where good manners would prohibit even priests from praying aloud: a whole complex of buildings and sites that would give expression to the sublimity of contemplation and a stepping aside," Nietzsche wrote in 1882 in *The Gay Science*.

I fundamentally believe that gentleness can bring exchange. It creates a space for silence in a field of speech, as well as time for understanding. It prompts us to ask ourselves what needs to be done so that a link exists and is created. It involves the other, and therefore the milieu. If the exchange does not take place, then gentleness serves no purpose. Being gentle, only for oneself, doesn't seem to be really useful. In the projects we develop, we always try to develop a dialogue with what is not working, precisely in order to structure through gentleness. We don't try to disappear into the part of the existing context that doesn't work, nor do we try to isolate ourselves from it, nor do we try to exhibit it.

This need to think of space in this way, beyond signs and noises, the space of silence, comes to me from the power of the sea. I think that silence is quite simply the present. Maybe that's why it's so frightening. Just like an unexpected event or an accident that intrudes into a day, it suddenly brings us back to reality.

Without silence, I think we cannot evolve. It enables us to listen, to learn about the present. For the architect, this is fundamental. If we don't listen to the present, that is to say to the milieu, if we don't realise how lucky we are to feel the real world, gentleness, the sun, the vital things, I don't know how or in what conditions we can make people live.

How do we look at space nowadays and at that which charges space?

Space can be understood as that energy that remains in us after we have passed through a place and that we leave when we pass through it. It comes from a primary function of exchange and breathing between life and the world. This is a "terrestrial" space, in the sense that Bruno Latour speaks of it. This dimension of the terrestrial in thinking about space gives things a steadfast quality.

The continuity between "nature" and our interiority may have been neglected in the transition to modernity. We isolated ourselves. We broke off the exchange. But then, what passes through us? Has our space not been fundamentally impoverished, as our ability to talk about the things that pass through us?

That's why I think we have to relearn to let go, to lose, to let ourselves be surprised, to not control the world. That is when we can escape, take the plunge, free ourselves. We have to learn to accept risk again, to accept dizziness, to escape, perhaps, from our anxieties. As an architect, I try to build devices for the resident's escape, liberation and imagination. In this, architecture can help us to heal a little.

In architecture, the devices that enable us to loosen our grip on things are, paradoxically, materialised by this idea of being attached to the world, the present. Architecture, in this sense, perhaps has the power to calm collective anxieties, whether it is a question of individual housing or public space, because it can do away with the obstacles and constraints around us. I think that, fundamentally, architecture has the power to bring us back to life. Its concreteness, the movements it activates, what it touches within us, help us connect to the reality of the present.

What is it that causes a space to liberate us? The fact that we can or cannot find release when we are in a given place? How does being in this space enable us to be somewhere else? If we place the resident in a situation of the present, of the unexpected, of equivocation, of limitlessness, we may well be able to reach these states of grace through architecture. In order to let oneself go, one has to accept that one has no control over anything. Architecture helps with this renunciation. And as long as you think you can control things, you remain in a state of anxiety… Letting yourself go means letting space pass through you. In this way, architecture touches on the deep questions of being in the world.

This question of unpredictability as an essential component of a project has always featured strongly in your work.

I have understood for a long time now that you don't control anything, you never do. That seems obvious to the entire planet today!
This premise, which has been clear to me since my childhood, forces us to open up to the world and to consider all constraints as opportunities for design. It forces us to trust, to be constantly willing to abandon our expectations, and to believe and design also with chance. This is how I practise as an architect. We try to express this notion of unpredictability through our projects.
It's a way of working from very early on with the site, the programme, the clients but also with space. I always leave a margin and a space between things. It's my way of embracing the unexpected, encouraging it to enter and anticipating the trouble it causes. This margin is not a leftover. It is a space

in its own right that holds the condition of new potentials. The added value of a project, the success it enjoys and the inexplicable pleasure it gives results, in our opinion, from this factor of unpredictability. It opens up an alternative history for the resident. It creates the capacity and potential of the project, beyond what is already there. The residents, the actors of the project, then may—or may not—make use of this intermediate and undefined space. It no longer depends on us, but the potential is there. Each project thus leaves a little to chance, like so many possible openings, new perspectives and reconsiderations.
It is very difficult to integrate—and make people accept—the notion of unpredictability in the project conditions as well as the notion of indeterminate space. This goes absolutely against how our modern economy and our relationship to the world functions. However, I think that these factors are key to a good project. This leap, this space interests me. One must understand that you can find elsewhere and otherness in the unexpected, and that this is a lesson for us all.

The composer John Cage wrote: "Structure without life is dead. But life without structure is unseen. Pure life expresses itself within and through structure." What purpose does structure serve in your projects?

I find this idea very moving!
In my opinion, the question of structure is related to the question of life and uncertainty.
As it happens, the epidemic we are currently living through is causing us to experience uncertainty, a feeling that France has not known since the last world war. Up to now, we let ourselves think that we were getting close to a zero

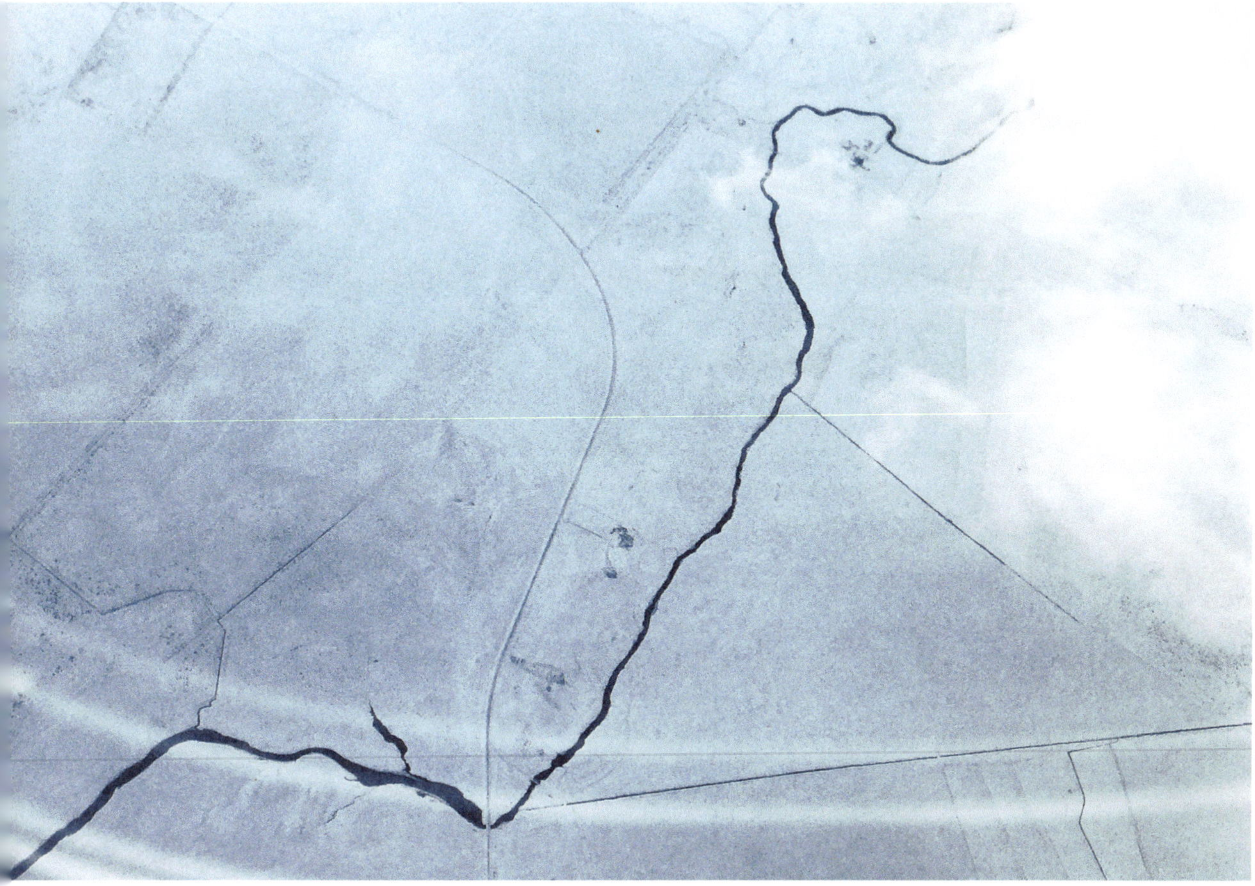

risk of instability, like an achievement built up and acquired over time thanks to diplomacy, guarantees, public health, prevention, etc. This belief has always shocked me. I have always found it implausible for anyone to be sure of anything. Since my childhood, I have known that nothing is really certain, and that any balance is necessarily unstable and shifting. This way of thinking is shared by everyone in Lebanon where, obviously, there are no structures to reassure the country's citizens. The fundamental awareness of movement and change is anchored in our minds. We know that we can never rely or rest on anything and that we must find arrangements that allow all the interdependencies to function together and support each other. This implies the participation of all essential components of human society.

One may wonder how a country like Lebanon holds together: it holds together by the force and energy that exist within and between people. But there is no real structure. There is only human life, the commitment of each person, but nothing supports this individual and collective energy wanting things to hold together. This condition, which is hard but perhaps free, tragic but sometimes magical, is a lesson on the importance of structure, its impact, its mode of presence and on what it can bring out or stifle in terms of human energy.

The importance of structure is raised in all our projects from the outset. We never work on structural issues after thinking about the project; it happens simultaneously. As an architect, I believe that a structure must liberate users, free them and not limit them. The main function of a structure is to connect people while at the same time detaching them. It is a fascinating system of interaction. That's why a structure is necessarily in motion. It must show that there are no limits between us, nor within us. Working on architecture through structure is ultimately what forges the connections and cohesion of the project. And this structure must not assert anything about the way the world holds together, how the world works. In my view, a structure must necessarily ask questions.

And at the same time, a structure makes it possible to return to a form of nativity, an archaism that refuses reference. When designing the Villa T, we did not want to add material, code or language in addition to the structure. Structurally, this villa behaves like a turtle. The structure makes inhabitation possible. It makes architecture. And, simultaneously, as expressed in its raw state, the structure expresses fragility. The same goes for the Villa M located on the heights of Beirut, on the side of an extremely steep slope. When you look at it from the road, you have no idea how this house is attached, or how it maintains its balance. It gives an impression of perpetual instability and risk. It's important for me to not reassure with the structure, to not express everything. Its hidden, secret dimension also proposes an interpretation of the world.

Thus, each structure we design contains a great potential for evolution and reassessment. In our opinion, a structure must allow for change. It must evolve and adapt. It is a living system. Its movements are internal, invisible but perpetual. For the design of Villa T, we took a lot of fluctuations into account in calculating this structure, because the magnitude coefficient was high, the cantilever was deep, and the glass panels were large.

We never design the structure of a project to be demonstrative. We always seek to express an escape and a form of fragility, of concern. This incites a reflection on the need for interdependencies. A structure cannot exist alone. It is a heterogeneous whole. In architecture, it represents a collective. This is all too often forgotten. It is not an entity that imposes its authority but a delicate set of fragments of construction, points, surfaces, articulations and assemblies in a state of transmission. It acts as a vector for many parameters related to the milieu, the ground, the wind, light and materials. By definition, it is attentive to the existing context. It must respond to external and internal factors collectively, but it is never finished or fixed. This makes things interesting for an architect. A structure holds things together because it is alive. It allows human life to happen.

What attitude to the project and what relationship to space does this approach to structure bring about?

When I have a new project, I start by hollowing out a space. First, I draw a void. I try to place the person, the encounter, the potential for exchanges and relations in the foreground. I try to create "holes" so that something happens. Carving out, rather than filling in, allows for connection and silence. Hollowing out is also a way for me to find that state of anteriority that I'm looking for in each project. As if, fundamentally, architecture is always an anterior state, a state that precedes us. Architecture, in this sense, is a new beginning, an already loaded whiteboard.

A hollow enables you to leave room. A hollow has no limit. It offers conditions for invitation. It opens up from the inside. It is a way of looking, of constructing the world and space. It is a way of looking for the other, complementarity, interlocking. That's why I like to design spaces that are never finite, never finished, never limited. I like to imagine spaces that are waiting for something. I like to construct fuzziness. This is what is most meaningful to me.

The site of Petra in Jordan appeals strongly to me in this respect, but also the church of Saint Pierre de Chaillot in Paris, which is simply a hollow mass traversed by light. This light allows us to break free of limits and project ourselves into a space of another nature. The Petra site teaches us how a raw material can become soft and habitable. How do we inhabit and become one with a cliff? What is more important, the cliff or what has been excavated? Or both together? In Petra, there is this very intense double situation, and around it, the desert…

In seeking to hollow out, I seek to construct the conditions of a milieu. By milieu I mean the space where energies and movements meet, the space of understanding, poetry and silence. In Lebanon, where there is no longer any interior, this is an important undertaking. We have to rebuild milieus, possibilities of thinking. Because we no longer have a milieu.

Starting from the milieu is an opportunity to open up to the unlimited, to get away from immediacy and excitement, to bring back stability, and to shift the debate. Building milieus is, paradoxically, a form of decentring when everyone else is focused on filling in or replacing. It is an opportunity to belong to something bigger, to escape from the interior.

As an architect, I like to work with the existing energy in milieus. Energy is the very flow of space, its heartbeat. I always try to understand it, to tap into it, to intensify it, to reveal it. Why do we talk so little about energy in architecture? Outside of any question to do with form, culture or material, to speak of energy is to speak of the elementary, the primitive.

When we were designing the Villa SC in Lebanon, in a village high in the mountains, energy was what drove the project, starting with the energy of the client, who was so particular,

whose footsteps barely touched the ground when he moved. I sought to build a space from and around this individual energy and to mix it with the very powerful energy of the site, of the void. I conceived this house as a "cape" that wraps around a body and a head. This large garment was imagined as a means of amplifying the territory. When you go inside this house, the site seems stronger, more intense, more powerful. I have experienced this phenomenon in the desert before. If you drape yourself in a piece of fabric, a robe, then you feel the desert even more. It is a strange phenomenon, precisely because it is linked to architecture's capacity to transform us. In the desert, the architecture is the robe around you. In this high mountain village, the architecture is a large, sensitive, open, and porous stone cavity.

When you put on a robe, why does the desert seem stronger?

Perhaps because you are naked, in an elemental state facing the desert, and therefore receptive to the milieu acting on you. Then the robe becomes an entry point. And this entry point has the power to include and connect you. The robe is the space of exchange, of the passage of energy. It makes this exchange possible, it is a breathing envelope that suddenly connects you to a milieu.

The robe is also a way of becoming aware of the relationship, of becoming aware of the desert and consequently, of dialoguing through the body. Thanks to this robe, you realise that you are connected, that you are entering into an exchange with a milieu. A work of architecture can have the same power as this robe we are talking about. It is a very powerful tool of awareness. In the Villa SC, the architecture simultan-

eously reveals two presences: that of man and that of the mountain. This simultaneity activates the relationship of exchange between the site and the body, each in its totality. It is very difficult to describe a landscape. You quickly become imprecise or lose track. Whatever you say, it remains indefinable. But if, all of a sudden, you place a piece of architecture, you focus, and you pin it down. It is by specifying it that you intensify it. This is an interesting dimension. Precision lets you render something present, I think. It lets you give a presence to something we would otherwise be unaware of and whose impact would be beyond our grasp. This state of presence through architecture produces an incredible emotion. Perhaps because architecture allows us to become one with the landscape, to internalise it, to capture and absorb its deep energy. The robe in the desert or the house in the mountains places us in the present.
Entering a work of architecture places us in an active situation of relationship, with the potential to concentrate all our emotions and heighten them. Just like a work of architecture, a word can amplify a situation and make it stronger. Architecture acts on us like a text. It has the power to detach us, to carry us away while also grounding us. Like the robe or the house, a word also embodies this possibility of exchange.
I fundamentally believe that things become stronger when humans are in a situation of sharing. This is our condition. The act of building is above all an act of linking and seeking out the meeting point between the individual and the collective.
This also pertains to a way of thinking about space in terms of "layers". This idea of "layers" touches on something fundamental in me. It means that things don't stop, don't limit themselves and that they are superimposed. It is a dynamic of perception.

In our project to redevelop the Bruneseau district between Paris and Ivry, this question was crucial. The site is very dense and intense. We wanted to avoid creating a frontal or immediate relationship between residents and the city. This intention completely modifies the very idea of the façade. In the residential tower we are designing, the layers exist through spatial devices—a bench, a ledge, a bathtub, a shift in scale. They add depth to the relationship to the outside and thus make an active interiority possible.
They create conditions for an exchange that an overly direct relationship would not necessarily have produced in such a context. They make it possible to generate something, to start a story where there is nothing.
We explored this for the Villa T near Beirut, but in a completely different form. When you enter the living room, the 13-metre cantilever of the concrete slab and the abrupt change in ceiling height allow you to move from a tight, even confined situation to a feeling of being fully open to the void. Without the use of a floor device or a wall, this idea of "layers" is nevertheless very tangible. The shift in scale here marks a transition and a change of state at the same time.

When you take a step back, how do you view your double experience of Lebanon and France today?

To approach this question, it is important to go back to the fundamental differences between the French and Lebanese situations. I am going to be deliberately a little general and exaggerate in order to clearly explain the prevailing trends in these two parts of the world that have, for me at least, led to quite distinct project experiences.

France, like the rest of Europe, is a largely industrialised country. This industrialisation of the act of building and producing is associated with a certain collective and centralising vision that aims to protect the greatest number, to foresee, to anticipate, to manufacture massively and rapidly, to develop and to progress. This of course has very significant consequences for architecture and the city. The urban planning that results from this approach is a political act, of public interest, occurring within a regulated framework.

Like France, Lebanon is dominated by the market economy but it is not an industrialised country. Industrialisation as a way of directing, generating or controlling is not collectively accepted or integrated. The state of war in which we have been embroiled for more than forty years has not enabled us to construct a shared and collective vision of the world or of the city. The government acts without a common vision and without a social project. The city of Beirut is a perfect example of this short-termist dynamic. In this context where the group cannot exist, the individual has taken over and is very powerful. The individual's room for manoeuvre is very significant because he does not have to conform to a collective vision. The individual does not depend on a system where everything is designed to fit together and be linked, where the framework is more impor-

tant than the individual. This situation allows one to live and act much more freely, in a way that is still "artisanal". It offers the individual a real ability to intervene in production, manufacture and creation. From the perspective of the act of building, there is no prefabrication in Lebanon and concrete is poured on site. Similarly, there is no industrial lobby. This is unthinkable in France! As for the influence of property developers, we still deal with individuals and not with groups. It is always possible to discuss and negotiate. This changes everything. We can therefore work on the project in a different way and design all its constituent parts. The architect can take full advantage of these margins of freedom. It also means that the architect has to anticipate everything, because nothing is really systematised, planned or well established in practice, which can be for the worst as well as for the best... Similarly, the rules are there to be discussed. The country is not legally precise enough to impose regulations. In France, the precision of the rules makes it possible to limit damage, ensure fairness, control energy, etc., but it is also a way of "formatting" the world. These differences between the two countries are fundamental.

What are the consequences of these fundamental differences in terms of practice?

The architect definitely enjoys latitude in Lebanon. You can get involved in the whole project chain and work closely with the craftsmen.
In contrast, in the French system, architects have little room for manoeuvre. Commissions are highly supervised, urban planning has a very big role, there's enormous

pressure from groups and lobbies, and the regulations are very rigid.

When I worked as an urban planner on the projects to transform the Brazza district in Bordeaux or the Bruneseau district between Paris and Ivry, I was lucky enough to get on board very early on in the first case, and in the second, to get involved in a situation that was so atypical—infrastructure, on the ring road, between two cities—that the developers were not able to take over from the start of the project. In both cases, we had to listen to each other and move forward together in a process of exchange and negotiation.

For the Bordeaux project, I tried to give real legitimacy to the unexpected, to open new doors in order to create a neighbourhood outside the generic mixed-use model: a piece of the city with different layers and scales in which the inhabitants can be actively involved. In particular, I tried to sequence the massing in order to avoid cutting up the buildings into macro-lots, to vary the housing typologies and contrast them, to propose a large number of "capable volumes"—surfaces with 5-metre ceilings left to be freely designed by the residents. I was able to do this because I came on board the project very early, at the beginning of the production chain.

Wherever I am, I refuse to be obliged to build quickly, I want to control the construction costs, the relationships with the companies and go back to what the material is really worth. This is an extremely difficult attitude to maintain in France.

I hope that the conditions of urban production in France will change. In the municipality of Bordeaux, they are beginning to reflect on the idea of slowing down the process of issuing building permits in order to think differently, to build less and less quickly. This is encouraging.

How do you deal with the question of "doing", which is once again becoming central for residents?

In France, the act of doing has been confiscated, in particular by the belief in the industrialisation of society, whose products, conveniences and services have seeped into our lives, particularly in urban areas. The act of doing has become a theoretical idea. It has been intellectualised to compensate for a lack of opportunities to do it physically. Yet, it seems that today we are all returning to this need to feel, to touch, to get involved in the making of physical space, whether habitat or public space. The health crisis we are going through, as well as the obstacles and frustrations that come with it, are making us perceive the finitude of the world. We feel it physically. We will have to accept this. The West cannot continue to believe in modernity. This transition we are going through is very interesting.
Whether it's about housing or urban planning, I think we have to return to the visibility of the production chain. While the Agora Biennial was taking place in Bordeaux in 2014, I visited a quarry in Ouagadougou where the entire production chain of public space was visible. Each inhabitant participated in its production and knew exactly where the material he or she was working with came from and how it had been transformed. Everyone had a very strong awareness of the city, of craftsmanship on an urban scale. They all belonged to a shared system of creation. This question, which is very much theorised in France, is not taken seriously enough in practice. I think that the relationship to appropriation, sustainability and the open-ended nature of the city and architecture depends essentially on the role we give to residents and citizens. This means giving up a certain culture of control and mastery in order to give residents freedom and trust.

This new situation brings up another point that is really important these days: the collective experience of the unpredictable. The pandemic we are living through all over the world has indeed affected all countries, in particular politically stable democracies where priorities seem to have shifted very significantly. In this respect, the health crisis puts us all on an equal footing and that is very interesting. We now share this common awareness that we are not in control of anything, whether we like it or not. Around the world this has given rise to a particular desire for universality, for simple emotions in physical space. Indeed, fear, anxiety, frustration and privation have changed people's priorities and ways of seeing things.
Due to the long years of war we experienced in Lebanon, people very quickly came to realise that unforeseen events offered opportunity. Opportunities to make things better. As soon as an opportunity arose, everyone knew to seize this chance to work and live differently. The slightest reversal could be transformed into an opportunity, a possibility.
And today, this notion of unpredictability is a strong bond between all Lebanese. Everyone has assimilated this "plan B" culture, the culture of making things work. The unforeseen teaches us that a new situation, as soon as we accept it, can become part of our daily life and become a project.
In France, we still don't think that an unforeseen event, an "accident", can be an opportunity. The whole organisation of the city and of society is geared to avoiding unexpected situations. But today, we are facing the most powerful unforeseen event we have ever known... And we are suddenly collectively linked to this same thing, which is the awareness that unpredictability is a reality in our lives.
We are probably entering a new era, the era of the present. And this is a new thing for all post-war generations. Anxiety

now exists worldwide. Governments are trying to reassure people, but deep down we have all changed. We will never be able to live or think the way we used to.
The strange time we are living in today is interesting from the point of view of territory. I think that a milieu becomes more important in times of uncertainty. Today, we approach the landscape, the climate and the sky differently because we are living with danger. A space gives off a particularly strong energy when humans feel anxiety or joy… I think that today we are collectively experiencing completely new dimensions in terms of openness, emptiness and milieu.

Villa M

Kornet Chehouane, Lebanon
2015–2018

Firmly anchored to the rock, the retreat in the mountains above Beirut had to fulfil many wishes. Youssef Tohme's response shows patience and sensitivity.

View from the living area, with the narrow walkway on the lower floor visible behind

Youssef Tohme Architects & Associates has completed a series of extraordinary private residences in the mountainous hillsides of Lebanon, each of which relates to a particular situation and idea that the architects took on, developed and then executed despite often challenging conditions. The Villa M is one of these, although in this case the client had very specific ideas of her own that proved demanding to elaborate into a suitable concept. The plot of land also presented its own challenges. Set on a steep valley hillside in Kornet Chehouane, a suburb of predominantly residential apartment buildings and villas scattered between the winding roads some ten kilometres from the centre of Beirut, the concrete block of the villa is only partially visible from the road. Only as one descends the broad ramp of the driveway behind a screening wall does one become aware of its true size below street level. The rectilinear exposed-concrete block can be seen as an architectural continuation of the rocky terrain but at the same time its monolithic form and different-sized openings set it apart clearly from its natural surroundings. From outside, the building's logic is not readily apparent.

Next page: **Building site showing the complex structural construction anchoring the new building to the steep slope**

The entire front of the large living area opens onto the valley.

The only direct access from the road is a wide, slightly sloping bridge that spans over the driveway and provides access to a double garage on the top level of the building. A door inside the garage leads directly into the hallway outside the villa's three bedrooms and is thus only for private use.
Visitors enter lower down from the driveway via a much more imposing entrance. After crossing a hallway with a long open staircase running the length of the building, they pass into the main living room which opens onto a spectacular view of the mostly wooded hillsides of the valley beyond. To one side, one can make out Beirut, the coastline and the sea in the distance. The entire structure is designed around this impressive view: there are no load-bearing columns, and entire panels of full-height glazing can be shifted to one side. The result is an ambivalent space that is at once sheltering and expansive—of the building and of the landscape. Strung along the front of this "belvedere" with its seamless indoor-outdoor transition is a remarkably narrow balcony with a balustrade of slender vertical bars.
The living area is designed as a largely open-plan space that divides at the entrance: to the left is a large dining area and to the right the kitchen

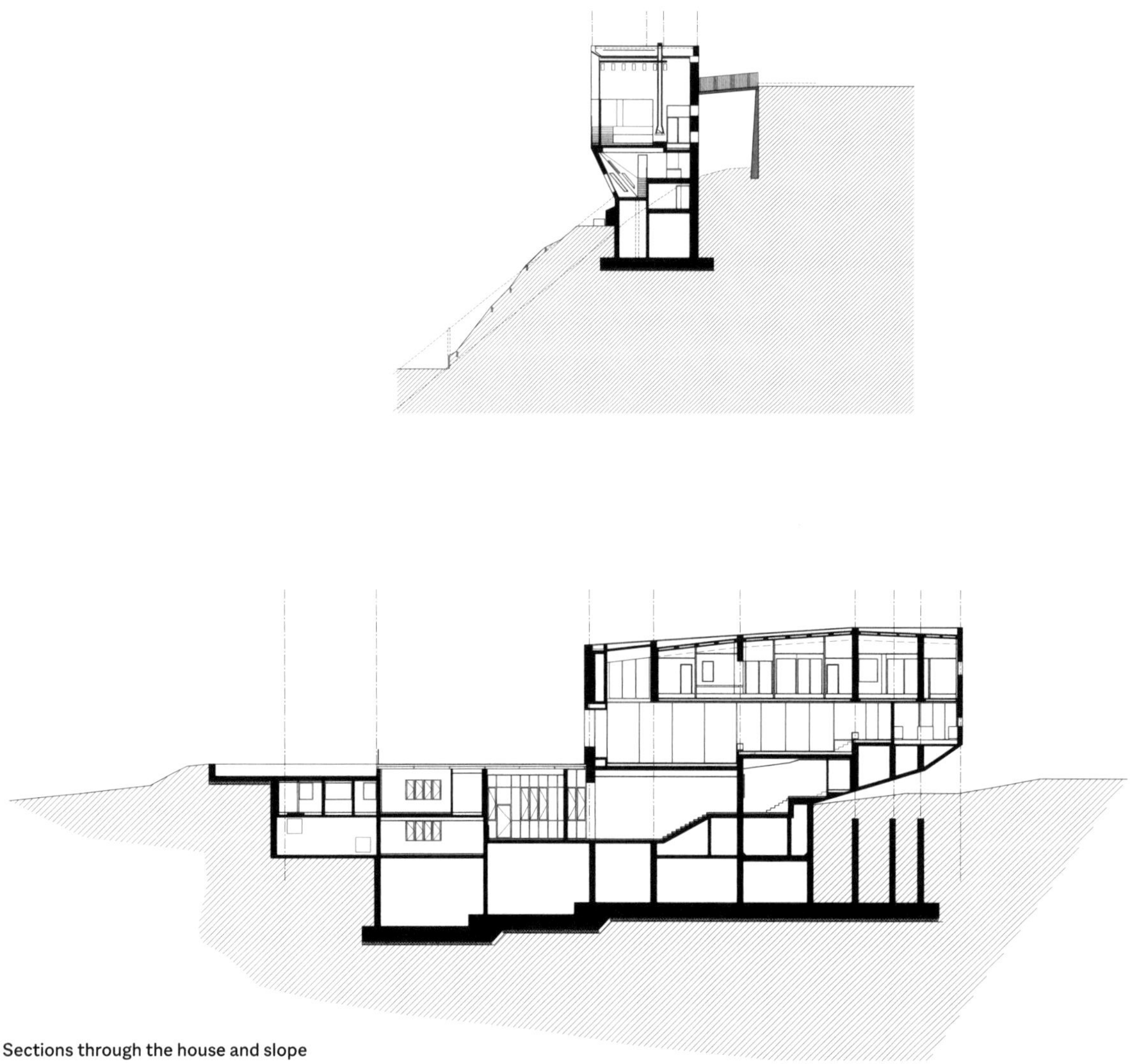

Sections through the house and slope

at the northwest end of the villa. The room tiers down twice, a flight of five steps and adjoining low wooden sideboards marking each change of level down to the fireplace and seating area at the bottom, which is a double-height space illuminated from above by a skylight next to the bedroom wing on the next level. Adjoining the southeast end of the house is an expansive terrace, a typical hallmark of the architect's work, which extends far forward of the depth of the house. Here, at the latest, one becomes a figure moving across a stage. At the landward side of the terrace, next to the driveway, is a more 20-plus metre-long and narrow swimming pool that disappears into a recess cut into the monolithic block of the building. One could almost swim directly up to the hall and stairs were it not for the fact that the water is very shallow at this point. In fact, the intention was that one can reach the pool from within the building via an open area with showers and a few steps down into the water.

The stairs and a lift connect the four levels of the building, including the technical facilities on the bottom floor, which also houses the water tank. The circulation is placed at the rear of the building but also offers surprising glimpses into the various spaces. Alongside the spectacular

The pool to one side can also be reached directly from within the house.

vista of the surroundings, the circulation with its flowing transitions between the spaces and outdoor areas is a further theme of the villa. As if this were not enough, the client had a special wish: she wanted the feeling of being "as free as a bird" overlooking the valley. The idea was that she could as far as possible "float" in her house. And indeed, the villa does appear to be perched somewhat tentatively on the site, although this only really becomes apparent when one looks down to see how it has been achieved structurally. To try to satisfy the client's desire to spread her wings, the architects devised the idea of a narrow, cantilevered concrete walkway on a lower level that extends out-wards more than eight metres above ground. It can be assumed that the suspended scaffolding necessary to support the formwork while casting this "footbridge to freedom" caused the engineers a lot of headaches, especially as they were already confronted with the structural challenge of anchoring the building in the rock. Next to a studio and a playroom below the large terrace is a second living area, principally for guests. Set apart from the actual geometrical block of the main house, its outer walls face into

The commanding view dominates the villa's architecture.

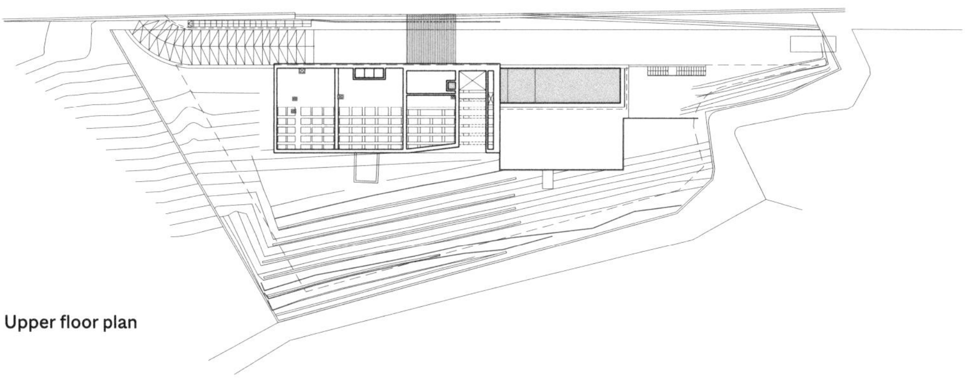

Upper floor plan

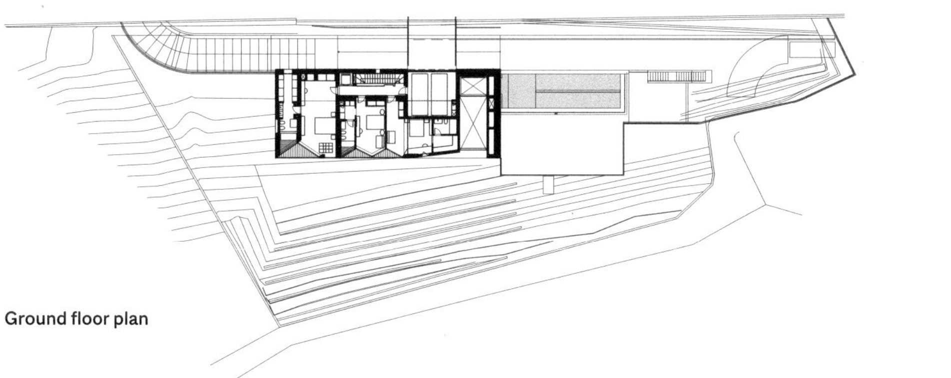

Ground floor plan

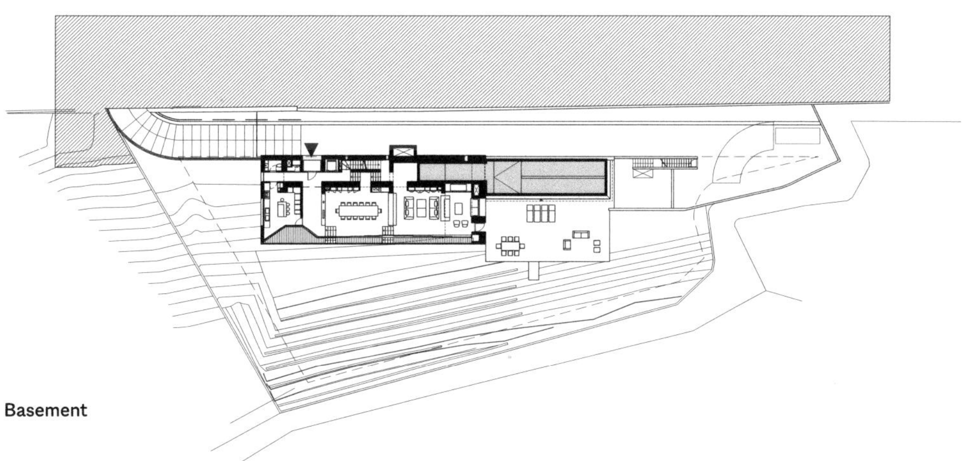

Basement

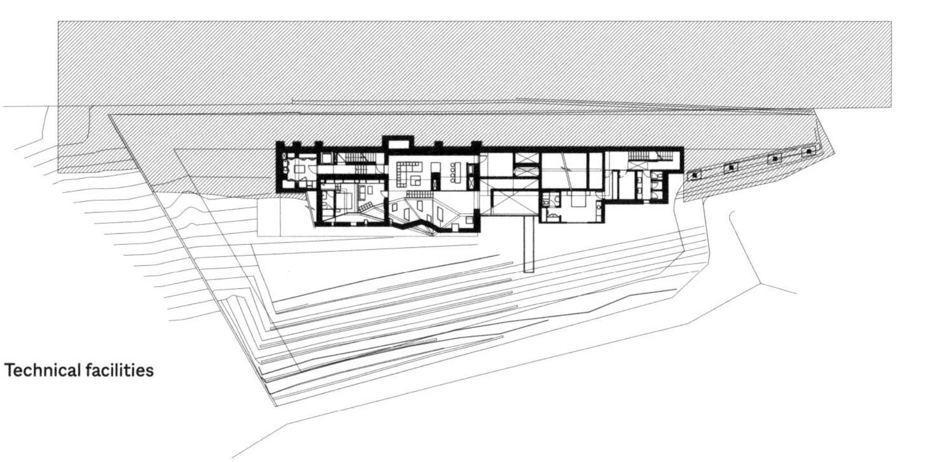

Technical facilities

Next page: **On the ground floor, facets of the outer wall slant dramatically outwards over the valley**

the valley and are broken into inclined faceted segments that look over the valley and have window openings of different shapes and sizes cut into them. One's perception of these spaces as well as their spatial quality is quite different to the rest of the house, and one has an impression of living between the supports of the main house. And indeed, the spatial composition is a response to the structural requirements that needed to be met. At the same time, it produces an interesting spatial tension: from within the safe vantage point of the interior and its solid materiality, one can lean out to look out of the windows into the vertiginous depths of the valleys. The combination of the oblique walls and windows and one's awareness of the weighty monolith overhead can have a dizzying effect. The interplay between the compact monolith and the expansive view it affords as well as the idiosyncratic idea of the plinth have all been realised with consummate finesse. This is a house in which one feels not calm relaxation but spatial stimulation.

Sebastian Redecke

The far end of the living area also extends upwards to the upper level.

Left page: **The villa appears to perch tentatively on the slope.**

Villa VR

Ajaltoun, Lebanon
2011–2016

In Ajaltoun, some 24 kilometres northeast of Beirut, stands another of Youssef Tohme Architects & Associates' hillside residences on an elevated site with spectacular panoramic views some 850 metres above sea level. Between the driveway off the road and the upper living area with the best views of the surrounding mountains is a height difference of 25 metres.

The villa sits atop an as yet undeveloped wooded slope overlooking the valley.

View from the lower plinth level of the rounded glazing of the living area

Next page: **View from the upper level over the roof of the living area and its shallow arcing rooflight**

The original design for the villa, which was completed in 2016, envisaged two main levels arranged offset and at right angles to one another, each capped with a large oversailing sculptural roof plane. In the office's visualisations they are shown as lightweight canopies that almost float above the sloping terrain. Both levels extend outwards and the upper of the two roofs can be reached via a broad stepped ledge that runs along one side. This core idea comes across with great clarity and elegance in the design visuals. The building itself, set back beneath the broad roof canopies, is at first barely visible. The main living area is an expansive space fronted by a continuous wall of glass with rounded ends that draws one in. Pushing slight forward out of the terrain, the swelling forms of the voluminous roof plane give the space a special tension. The arcing sculptural forms of the roofs shown in the initial designs have been successfully carried through to the final building and are even more dramatic as they are realised in concrete, the material mass of their exposed undersides defining the character of the living area. This breath-taking sculptural element is rooted in a grand symbolic gesture: that of embedding the building in nature with the silhouette of the mountainside. In the actual building, this aspect has lost some of its conceptual clarity and is not quite so clearly legible due to the dominance of the two roof surfaces.

In addition to the two main levels, the villa also has a partially subterranean plinth level that contains parking for seven vehicles as well as the staff living quarters, a laundry room, storerooms, technical services and the obligatory water tank. An entrance area and open bar greet visitors arriving on the main level, which comprises an

expansive open living area and adjoining dining room that open via the fully glazed frontage onto the terrace and pool area with the landscape as a panoramic backdrop. A suspended, rotatable black fireplace hangs from the ceiling. At the rear of these open salons are the ancillary spaces including the kitchen, a large fitness room, an office, guest room and a further parking space.
A flight of stairs arranged at right angles to the terrain leads upwards between two parallel wall planes that serve to divide the dining area from the rest of the living room. As in many of Tohme's other villas, this level with its open interior and expansive terrace is intended as a "landscape room", with the remaining spaces arranged behind it. On the next level, set back under a second roof, is a further living room and a series of four bedrooms arranged next to one another, the last of which is the larger main bedroom. Here the corridors are lined with wood panelling. As before, full-height glazing and a side terrace overlooking the terrain open onto the surroundings.
Given the voluminous interiors of the villa, it seems incongruous to speak of simplicity, but its interiors nevertheless exude a sense of simple clarity in that they refrain from opulence and ostentation. The spaces are simply conceived with a limited palette of materials, dominated mostly by exposed, light-coloured concrete. Ancillary aspects—and especially the complex technical services—are carefully concealed from view.

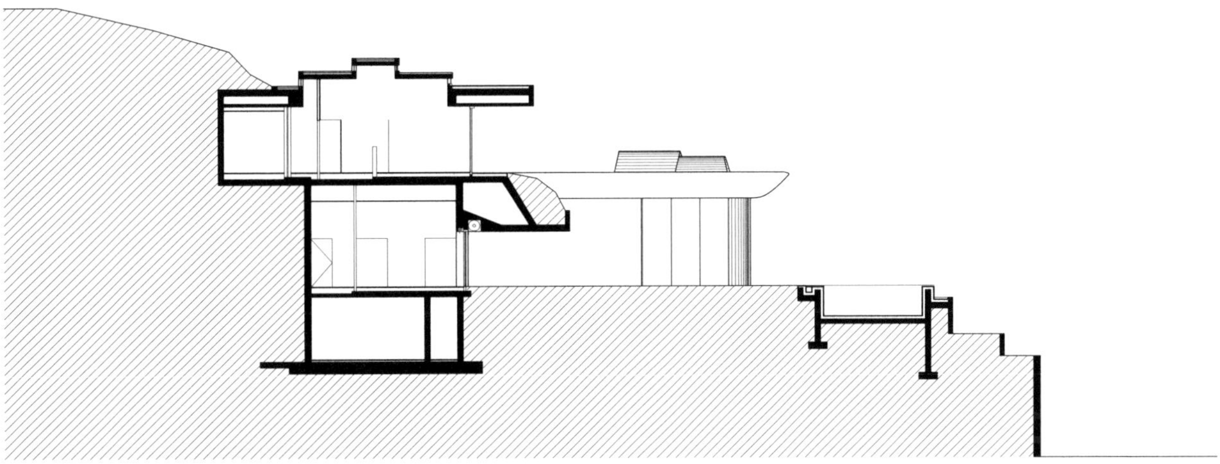

Cross-section through the three levels of the villa

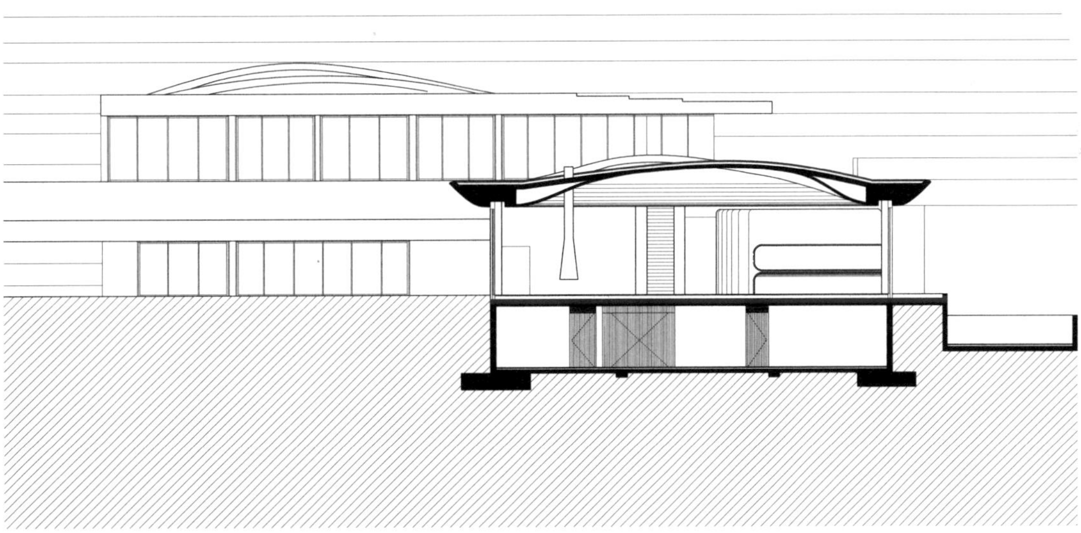

Sectional elevation parallel to the slope

Left page: **Curved, in-situ cast concrete shells lend the roofs a special quality.**

Next page: **The curved concrete shells define the character of the living area.**

What sets this house apart from Tohme's other villas in Beirut's mountainous hinterland is the theme of the roof form. It is inspired not just, as the architect describes, by the natural landscape but also by other wave-like, organic and voluminous architectural structures which he spans across the ceilings of the interiors. The irregular slits these produce in the roof surface allow light to spill into the room. In addition, the underside of the ceiling is backlit. Once again Youssef Tohme has pushed the boundaries of the material, challenging his contractors to realise structure of great precision requiring elaborate and complex formwork.

Alongside the cantilevered roof forms, it is the villa's spacious interiors and expansive terraces that are most impressive. Placed against the backdrop of the surrounding scenery, they could quite easily serve as stage sets. From outside, however, the building presents itself very differently: here Tohme has focussed on embedding the villa into the topography of the mountainous landscape.

Sebastian Redecke

The contrast between the concrete and delicate glazing is striking.

Left page: **The building site with the in-situ cast concrete roof and the pool in the foreground**

The wood-panelled corridor to the bedrooms on the upper floor

Underside of the ceiling above the corridor showing the glazed strip

Right page: A narrow staircase leads towards the light on the upper floor.

The dramatic entrance to the villa

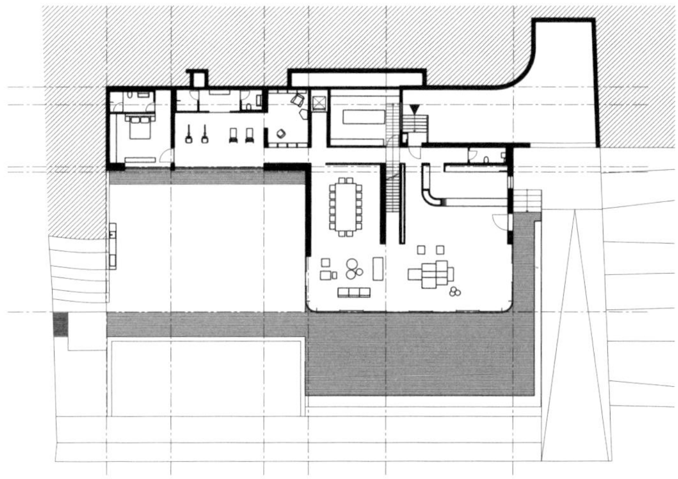

Top floor plan

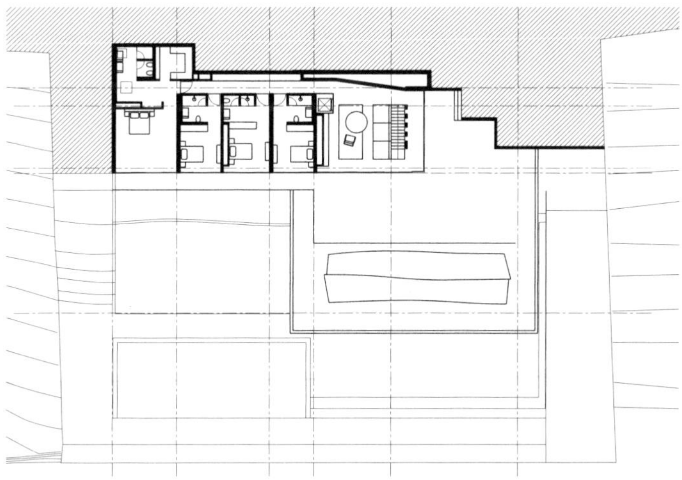

Upper floor plan

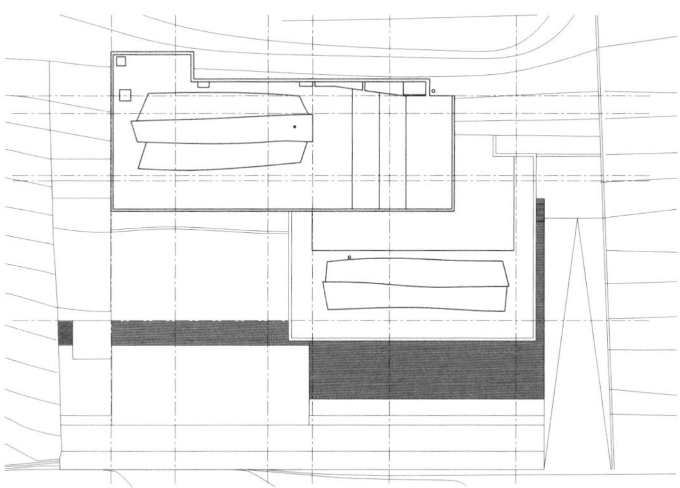

Ground floor plan

Brazza District

Bordeaux, France
2012–2030

In 2014, Youssef Tohme Architects & Associates won a major invited competition for the design of a new 53-hectare urban quarter for a stretch of landscape in the city in Bordeaux.

Designed as an "éco-quartier" with a strong focus on sustainability, the quarter is one of the development areas along the "Rive droite" on the east bank of the river Garonne that is being developed by the rapidly expanding Bordeaux Métropole municipal association. On the initiative of the long-standing mayor Alain Juppé, who was in office until 2019, the association has been working together with numerous architects, urban planners and landscape architects on the urban expansion for Bordeaux. An important and also striking link in the overall concept is the Simone Veil Bridge over the Garonne, designed by Rem Koolhaas/OMA. Construction of the bridge, which is intended to extend the Bordeaux waterfront, began in March 2021, and with a

The new urban district contains areas of small-scale mixed-use development.

width of 44 metres the bridge is designed to be wide enough to stage events on it.

The neighbourhood designed by Youssef Tohme in collaboration with landscape designer Michel Desvigne lies some three kilometres further north, next to the Jacques Chaban Delmas Bridge, a lift bridge construction which opened in 2013. The Brazza district derives its name from that of the road along the river, which is named after the French African traveller and naval officer Pierre Savorgnan de Brazza, who founded Brazzaville, now the capital of the Republic of Congo, in 1879.

The area had previously been occupied by small businesses and boat builders, but over time many of the production works and warehouses were abandoned until much of the area was derelict wasteland. The new quarter, which encompasses various innovative aspects, will contain a mix of buildings for living and working, with special focus on crafts and trades as well as cultural, educational and sports facilities. It will join up with riverside areas further south of Brazza that are already under construction.

Youssef Tohme's involvement with the city goes back to his role as curator of the Agora 2014 Biennale of Architecture, Urbanism and Design in Bordeaux, which focused on the theme of "Espace public" and hence the further planning of the city. The public forum addressed and discussed key questions of urban open space design and mobility in the context of Bordeaux's

Some buildings are raised off the ground on slender pillars to allow greenery to pass beneath them. The roofs are also greened for the residents to use.

major urban development projects, all of which are also central issues for the Brazza district. The overall plan will provide 4950 dwellings with a total floor area of 468,500 square metres. Four hundred ninety-nine of these are so-called "Volumes Capables" in which the residents acquire an open shell that they can then build out on their own to meet their respective needs. These are offered at the very low price of between 2100 and 2400 Euro/square metre for room heights of 2.50 and 5 metres. The intention of this architectural and urban design idea is to stimulate the evolution of a vibrant quarter with a self-determined and self-confident identity. Alongside these are 2097 flats in tower-like buildings with up to six storeys and wide wooden terraces. Raised off the ground by up to 5.5 metres on slender columns, they will allow the greenery of the district to flow through beneath the buildings. Four hundred sixty-five

Master plan of the Brazza District and the Jacques Chaban Delmas Lift Bridge

single-family houses of an almost rural character are incorporated into the master plan, divided by small passageways. Their design draws on the "Échoppes bordelaises", the typical two-storey houses that line the streets in much of Bordeaux, each house slightly different to the next. Car parking is grouped into specific areas and concealed by raised gardens.

A new tram line, the "Brazzaligne", follows the course of the former railway line and links the new quarter to the public transport network. Together with a broad green avenue, it forms the spine of the southeast end of the quarter. The buildings along this street are larger, five-storey-high constructions with additional, smaller-scale rooftop structures surrounded by terraces. These "Bâtiments Brazzaligne" contain a further 1357 flats as well as offices and shops and are designed to be adaptable to meet changing requirements. This "plasticité fonctionnelle", as Tohme calls it, is highly appropriate to today's needs. Several axes run crosswise to the spine and lead down through the quarter to the Garonne, where the recreational facilities of the Quai de Brazza and the Parc aux Angéliques adjoin the river. Here significantly taller buildings with up to 14 storeys are planned, set back from the water. Accommodating a mix of flexible uses, including more than 600 flats, these are designed to harmonise with the surroundings. The riverside development is subject to the "Charte Garonne", which defines the overall planning perimeters in terms of volumes, materials and colours to ensure a fitting overall silhouette along the waterfront. The transverse axes from the Brazzaligne to the quay, by contrast, are designed as narrow, paved residential streets, as bicycle paths or simply as green strips planted with poplars to serve as recreational ecological corridors for the residents. Poplar trees have been selected to ensure that sight lines are not unnecessarily obstructed. A total of 5000 new trees are planned for the entire area. The tram line also runs along one of these green transverse axes through the district. Car traffic from the Chaban Delmas Bridge, on the other hand, does not pass through the neighbourhood, but is turned north or south at Quai de Brazza.

A central goal of the project was to provide affordable housing in a location well connected to the city. The Volumes Capables in particular, as houses for independent development, aim to accommodate individual wishes and be spaces of possibility. Ongoing feasibility studies are being undertaken with the developers and in dialogue with all relevant stakeholders as part of the urban

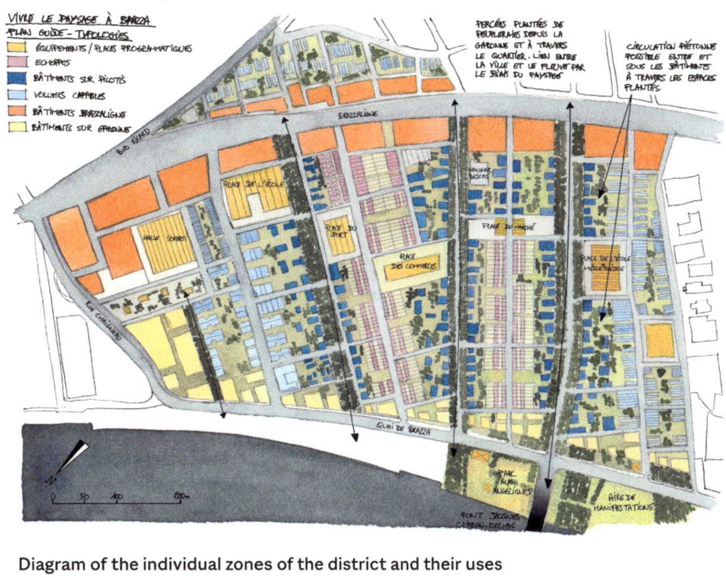

Diagram of the individual zones of the district and their uses

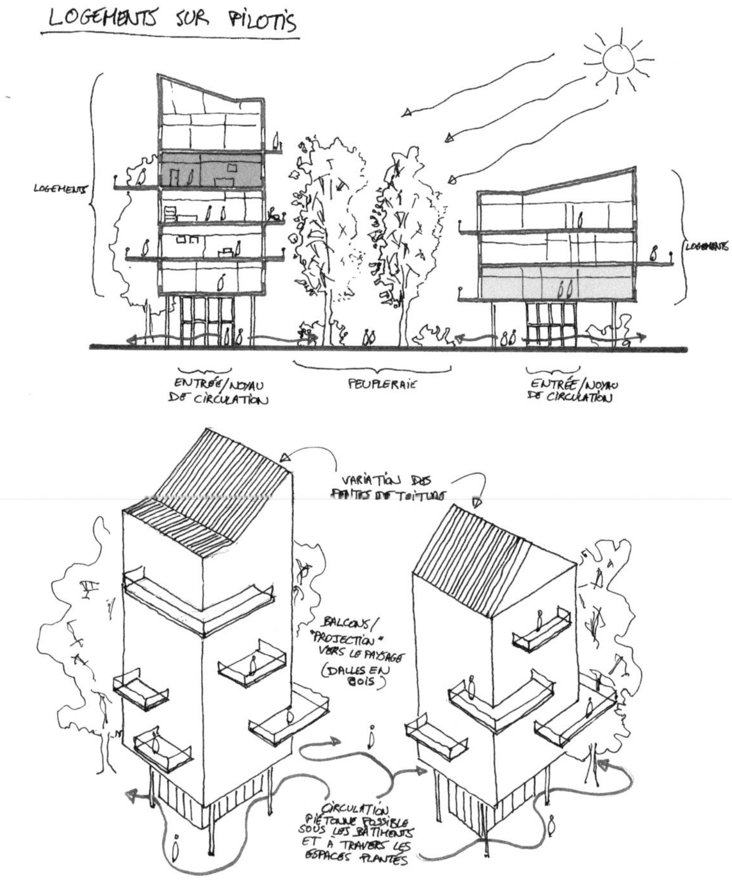

A tall building type standing on circular pillars with varying roof forms

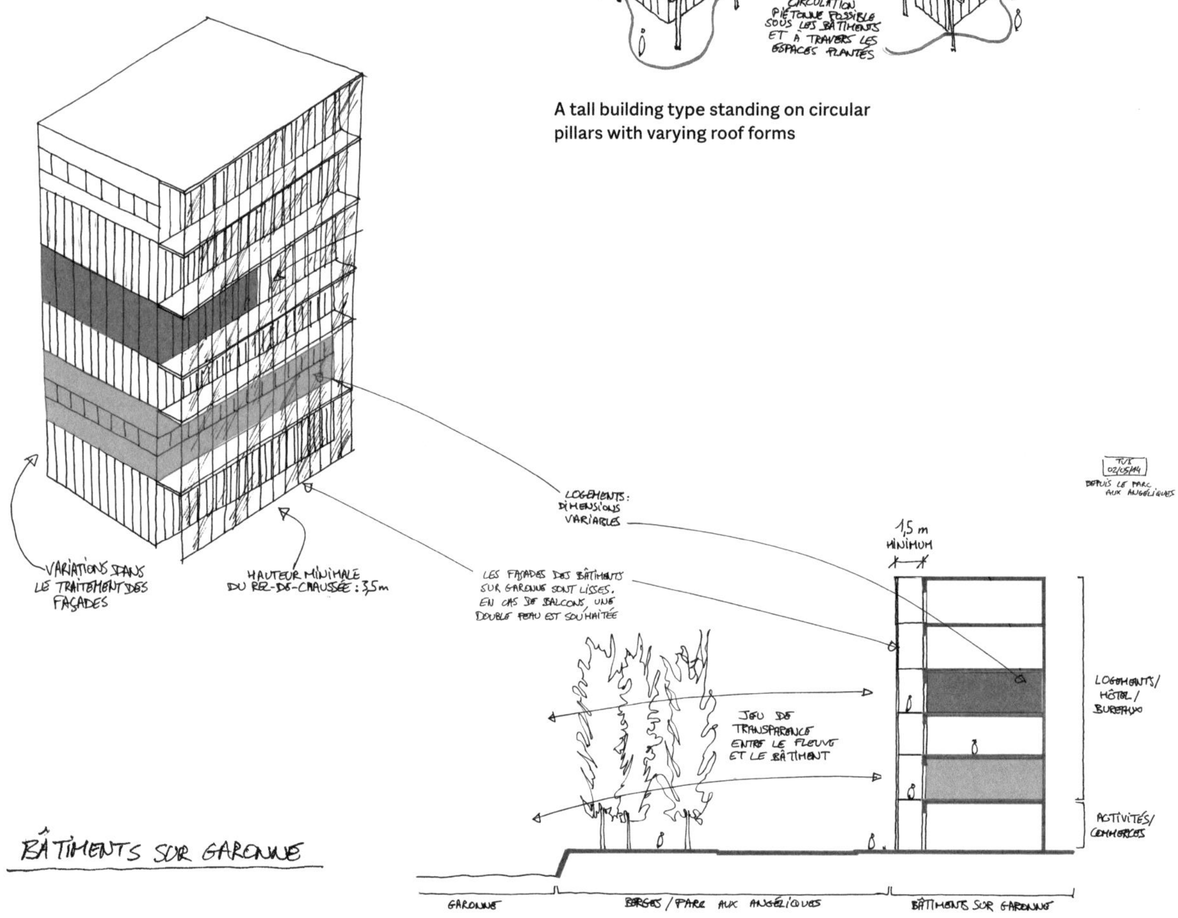

A large building type alongside the Garonne

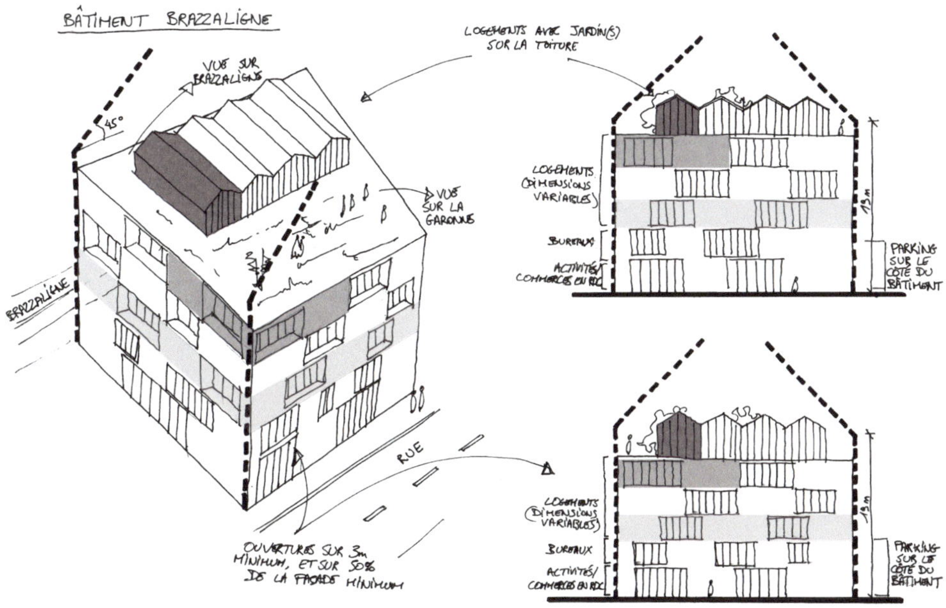

Building type in the main development area and adjoining the Brazza ligne spine

Broad green strips with some of the 5000 newly planted trees cross the Brazza District.

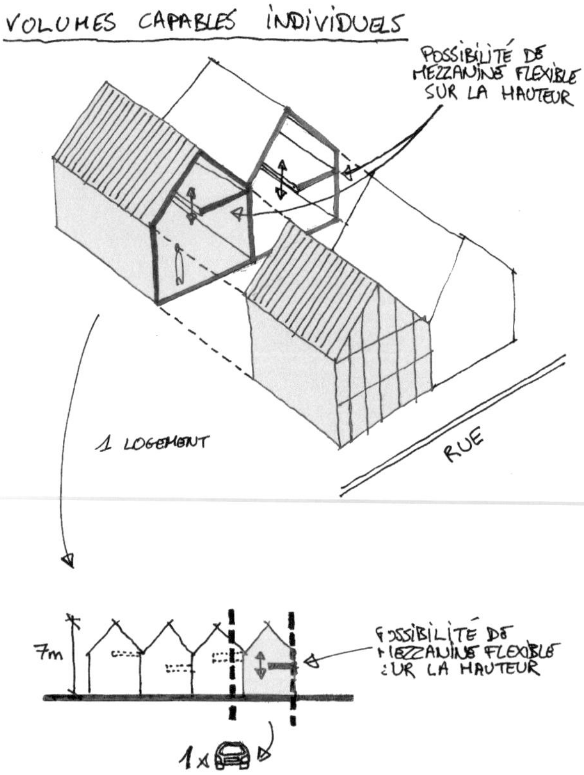

Simple building shell concept that can be extended by the later residents

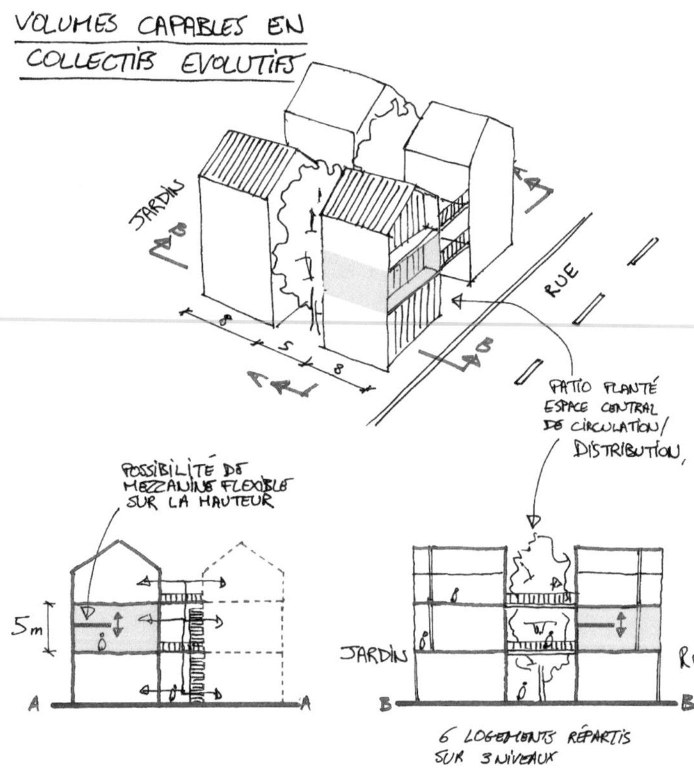

A building type that can accommodate varying uses

planning framework and the Atelier Brazza led by Bordeaux's Urban Planning Authority. Further participants are being involved in the development of cultural facilities. The district will be home to the "Cathédrale des Sports" sports centre as well as three school facilities. Geothermal and solar energy also play an integral role in providing heating and hot water for the district. The urban design takes into account the risk of flooding in the event of high water and contaminated soil, for example from a former fertiliser factory, will be removed. As far as existing buildings are concerned, selected structures have been retained, including the vacant Soferti Hall in the northern part of the urban quarter, an impressive wooden structure dating from 1904, which will be redeveloped and converted as a central location for commercial and cultural uses. Other existing buildings such as the Descas Industrial Works are still awaiting a new use. An old industrial chimney has also been retained as a symbol of the neighbourhood's history. Youssef Tohme's primary goals were to provide opportunities for a high degree of design freedom within a relatively small-scale urban order that skilfully varies in its rhythm and scale according to its location along the edges or within the district. Paired with a convincing interpretation of the garden city concept in which traffic infrastructure has been significantly slimmed down, the hope is that this can engender a positive social mix of different residents.

Sebastian Redecke

A central neighbourhood square with buildings for shops and businesses

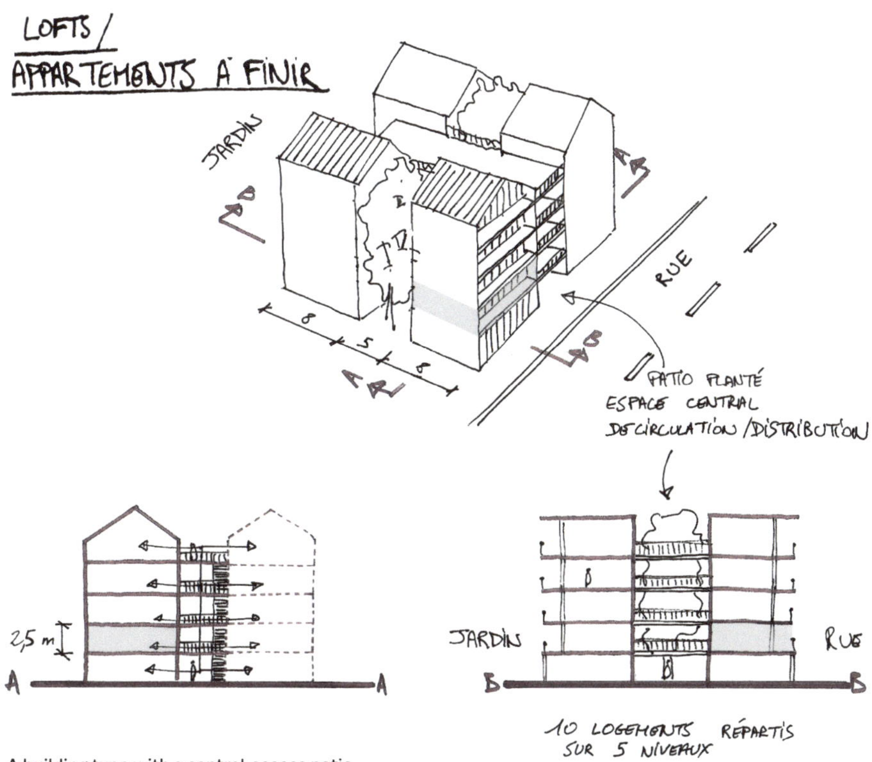

A building type with a central-access patio

Quartier Bruneseau

Paris, France
2018-ongoing

Between Ivry and Paris, in the Bruneseau district, infrastructure is architecture.

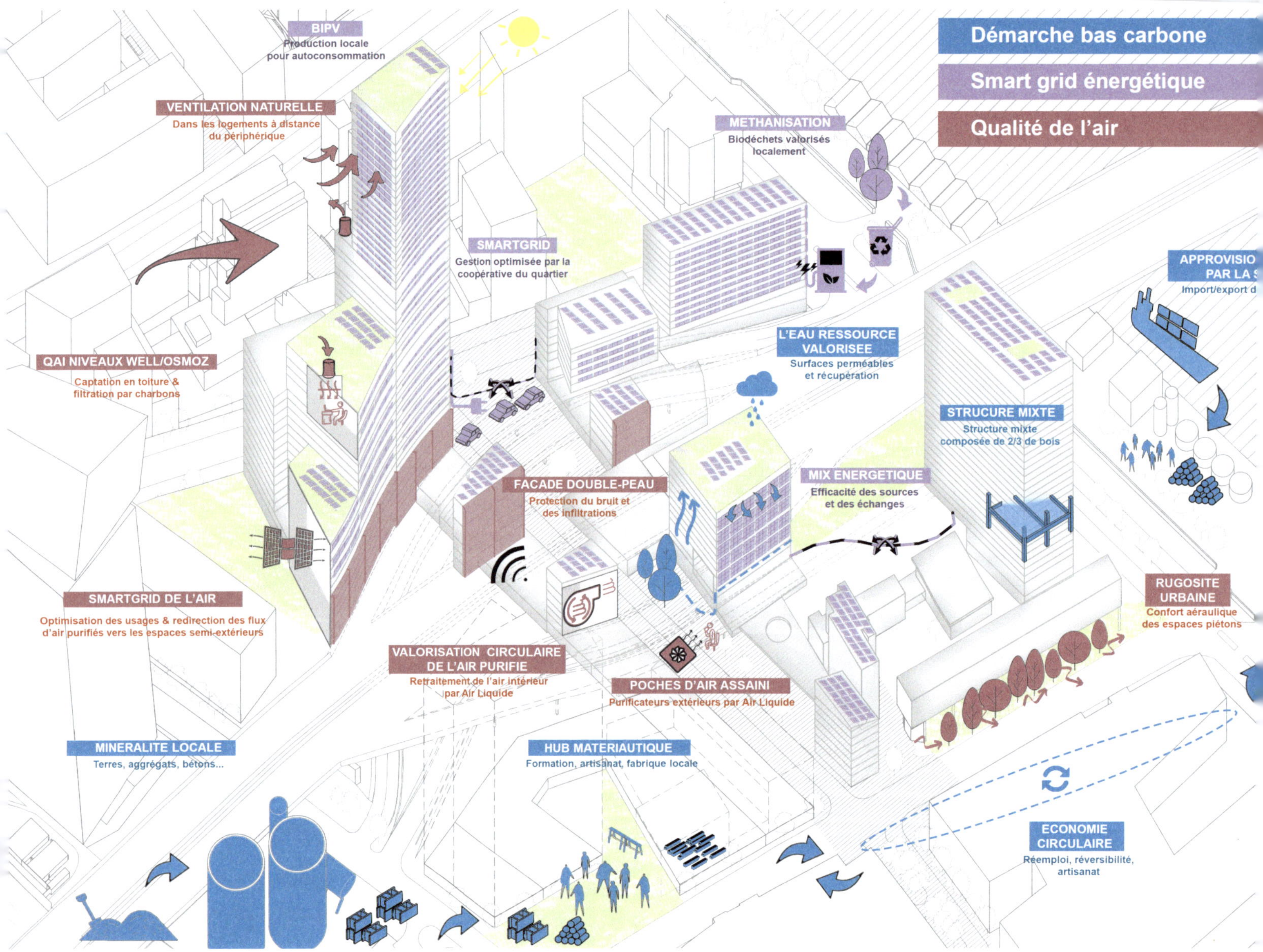

Energy diagram

The *boulevard périphérique* ring road offers a new potential in this location: an unprecedented opportunity to create habitat. The focus here is on transforming the gaze and reinforcing the transversality anticipated in the master plan. Envisioned as a highly fertile typological thickness going from ground to sky, the area covered by the elevated ring road becomes the vector of continuity and connection between Ivry and Paris: a milieu, an interiority. Against all expectations. This superstructure constitutes a potentially inclusive space, a new imaginary from which the project can begin. A peripheral milieu. Thus, the underside of the infrastructure, its surface, its ramps and its interstitial spaces liberate a new potential for the city, one that can neither be simplified nor reduced. As it is impossible to standardise, this spatial situation creates the conditions for exceptional generosity and openness, qualities that are essential for urban production today. This freedom acts as a catalyst for social and progressive thinking.

The piece of architecture formed by this portion of the infrastructure is associated with an open programme with a strong potential for practices, exchanges and mixed uses. Its topographical richness in fact sows the seeds of unexpected appropriations and scenarios. Viewed from the ground, the ring road thus becomes a Great Hall spanning the Paris-Ivry thoroughfare, an intensifier of uses, exchanges and invention. Explored on the surface by new forms of mobility, it begins its transformation into an avenue. Constructed and densified in its interstices, it is flanked by a series of vertical extrusions accessible to the public that frame the Paris-Ivry thoroughfare and form the crucial link between the lower and upper parts of the infrastructure.

The active tool making this tiered piece of city function comes in the form of capable structures: resilient and specific spaces, designed to evolve with use and to adapt to unforeseen changes. Thanks to their flexibility and their width, these structures provide non-standard conditions and grant a certain freedom. In the Great Hall, they forge links, protect and welcome, but also invent new limits between public and private space. Organised in clusters, they make us forget the road and extend horizontally towards Ivry until they reach the block of the Cité administrative: a condenser of living heritage, open to the emblematic actors of the city such as artists and craftsmen. In the extrusions, the capable structures offer the necessary thickness to create vertical fluidity and appropriation. Going up or down and entering must be as easy as walking and circulating.

And to make this device work, it is activated by human presence. In situations of this kind, untouched by prior uses, location and programme are not enough. Stimulated as connectors and aggregators, individuals can shape the space. This means residents, of course, users and visitors, but also the actors of community associations, entrepreneurs and developers. Today we need to create new alliances and new economic models to produce the city differently, and to learn how to make it evolve over time, to maintain it, based on humankind and the complexity of reality.

Thus, going against any idea of the city-object and zoning, a mode of urban generation made of negotiations, increments and transformations is developed. It responds to the specificity of a fragmentary and systemic city, comprising multiple parameters. A city is an equation that progresses: a system of free and continuous variations. The idea is to distribute the forces—economic, programmatic and human—and understand the speed or slowness of these forces. This approach calls for dynamics of financial equilibrium and steady progress: a completely new condition for development. Particularly relevant in situations of appropriation and invention,

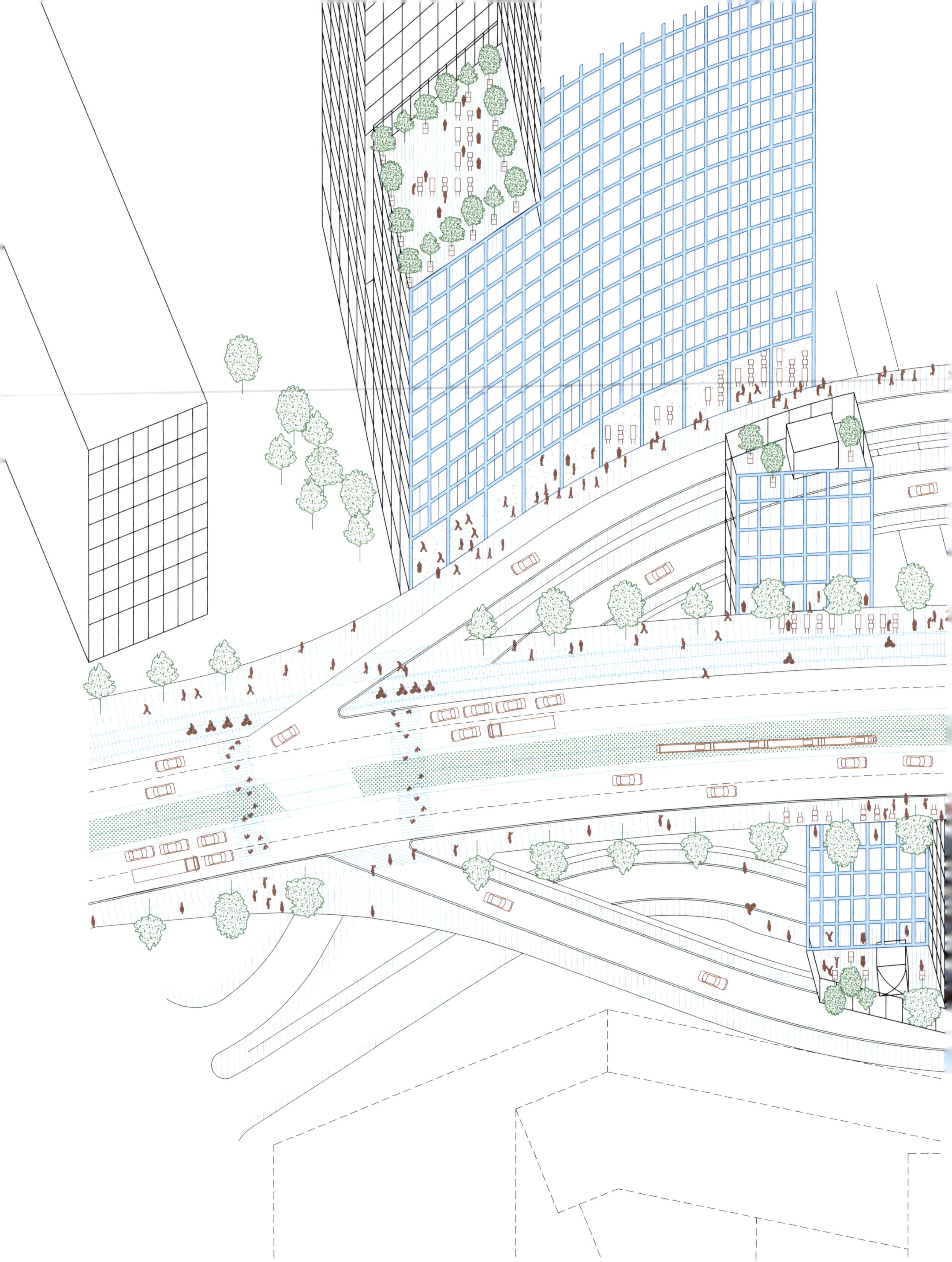

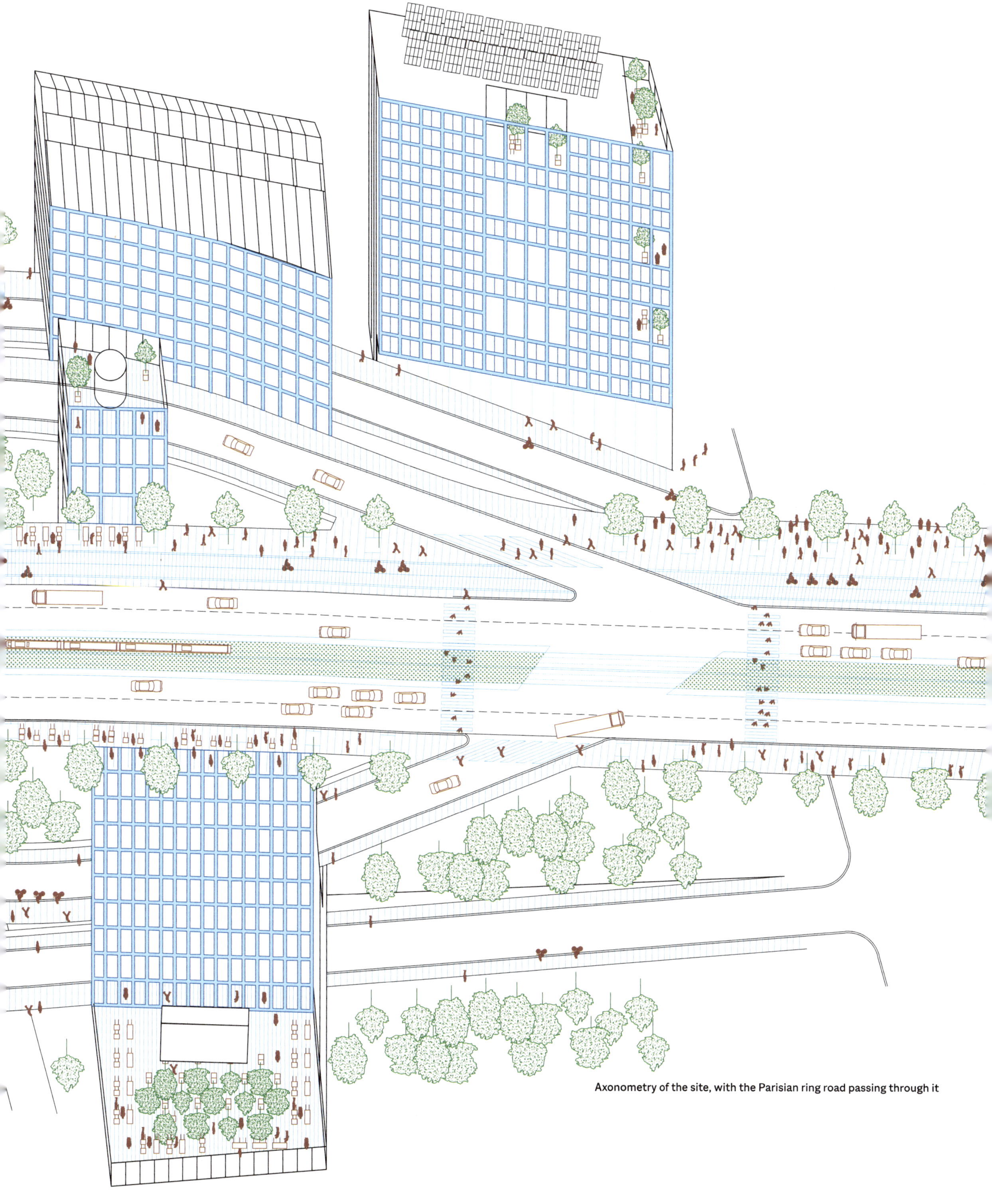

Axonometry of the site, with the Parisian ring road passing through it

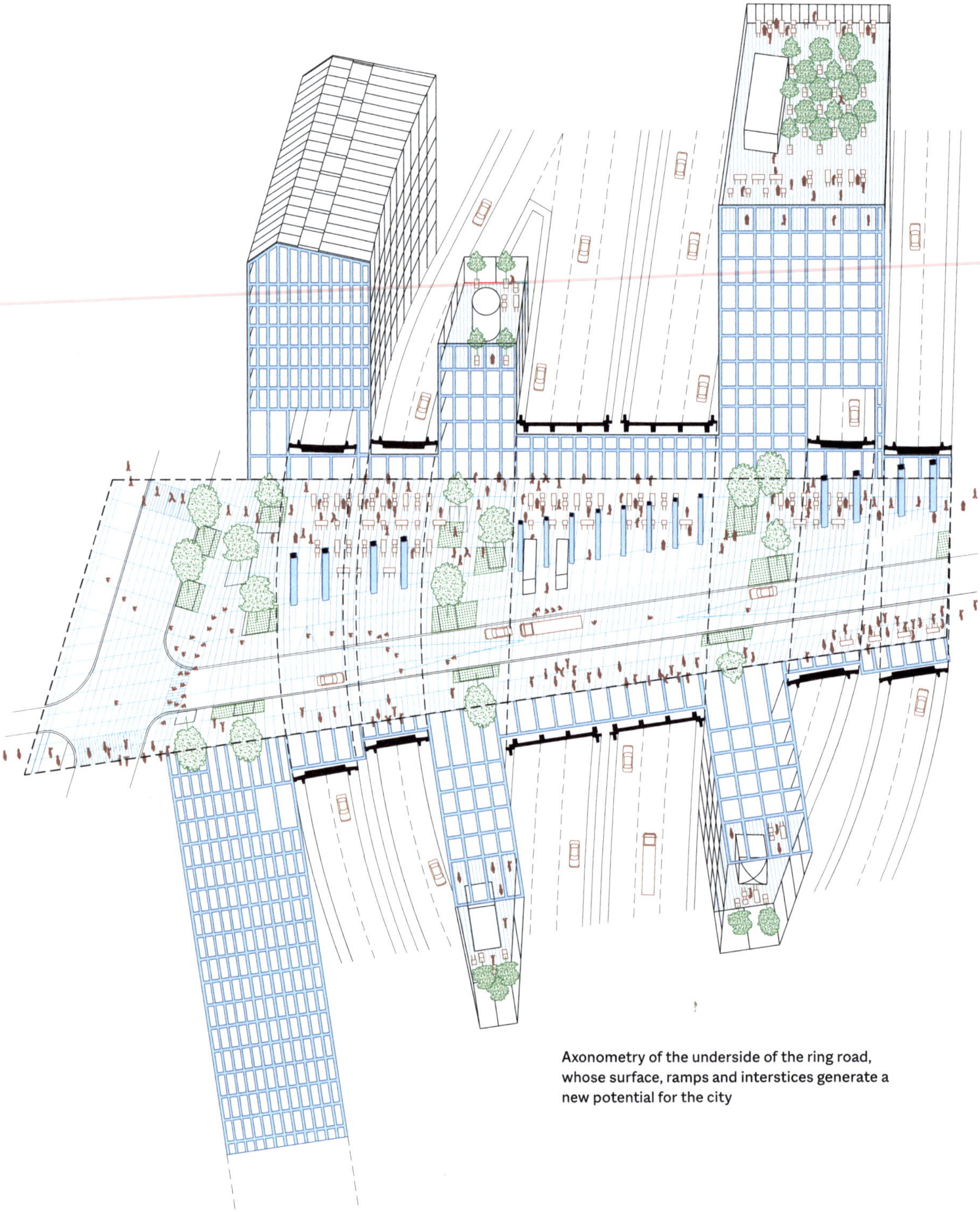

Axonometry of the underside of the ring road, whose surface, ramps and interstices generate a new potential for the city

Axonometric view of how the ring road, approached from its underside, becomes a large hall extending on both sides of the Paris-Ivry thoroughfare

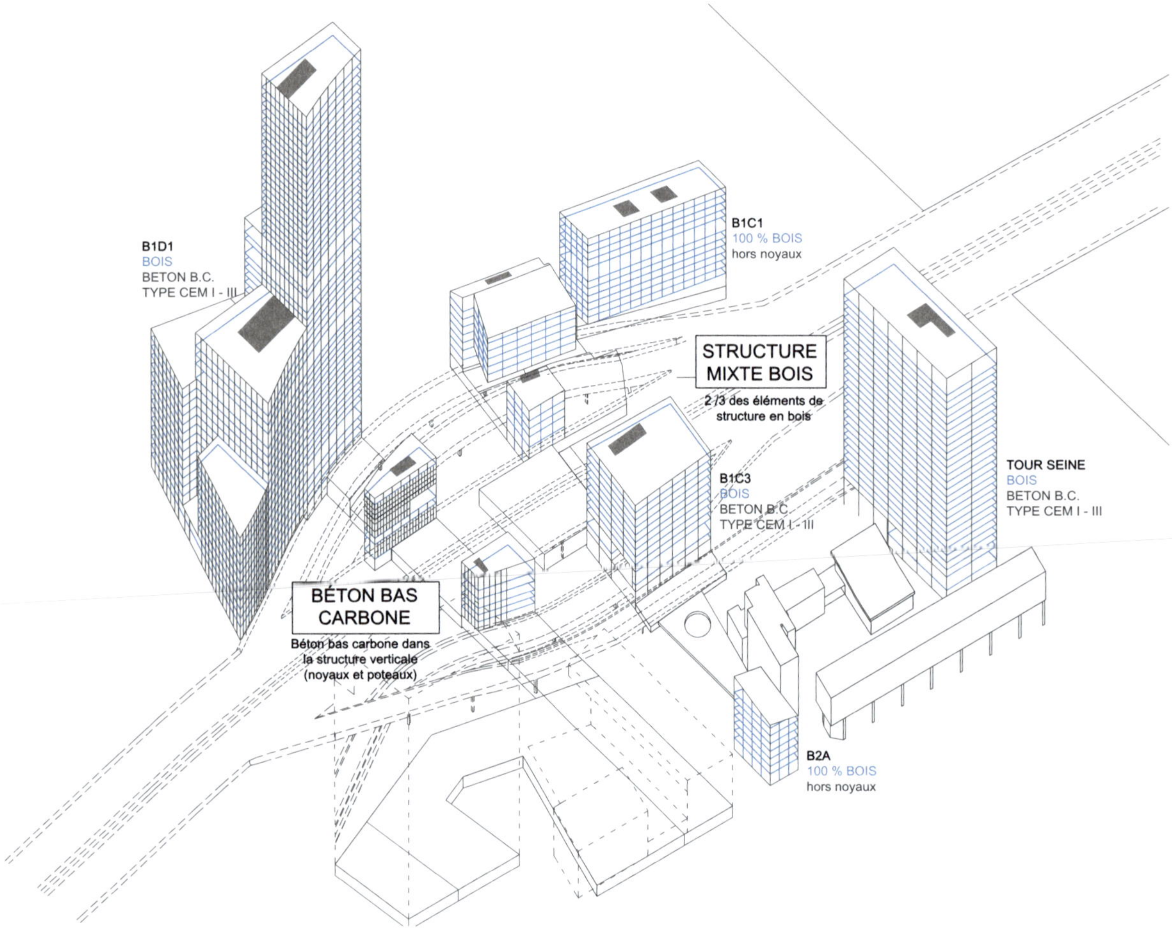

Organisational diagram

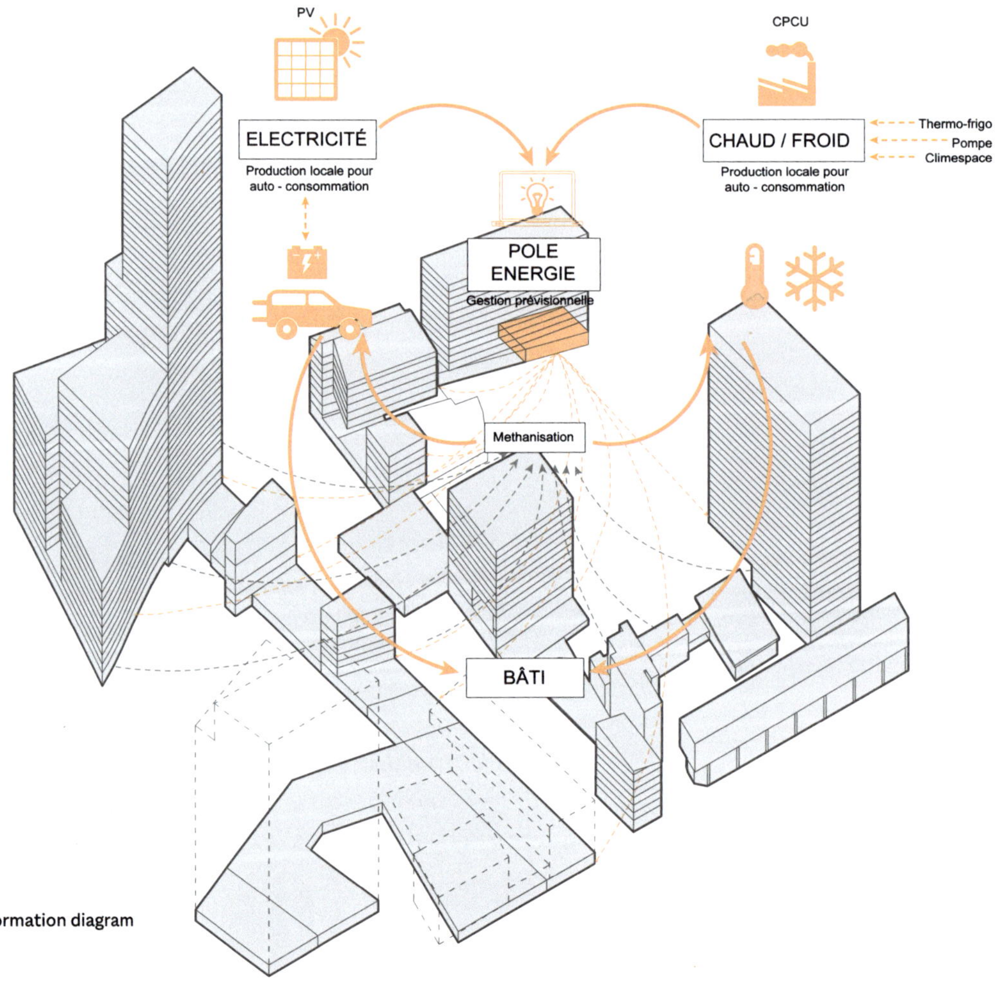

Energy transformation diagram

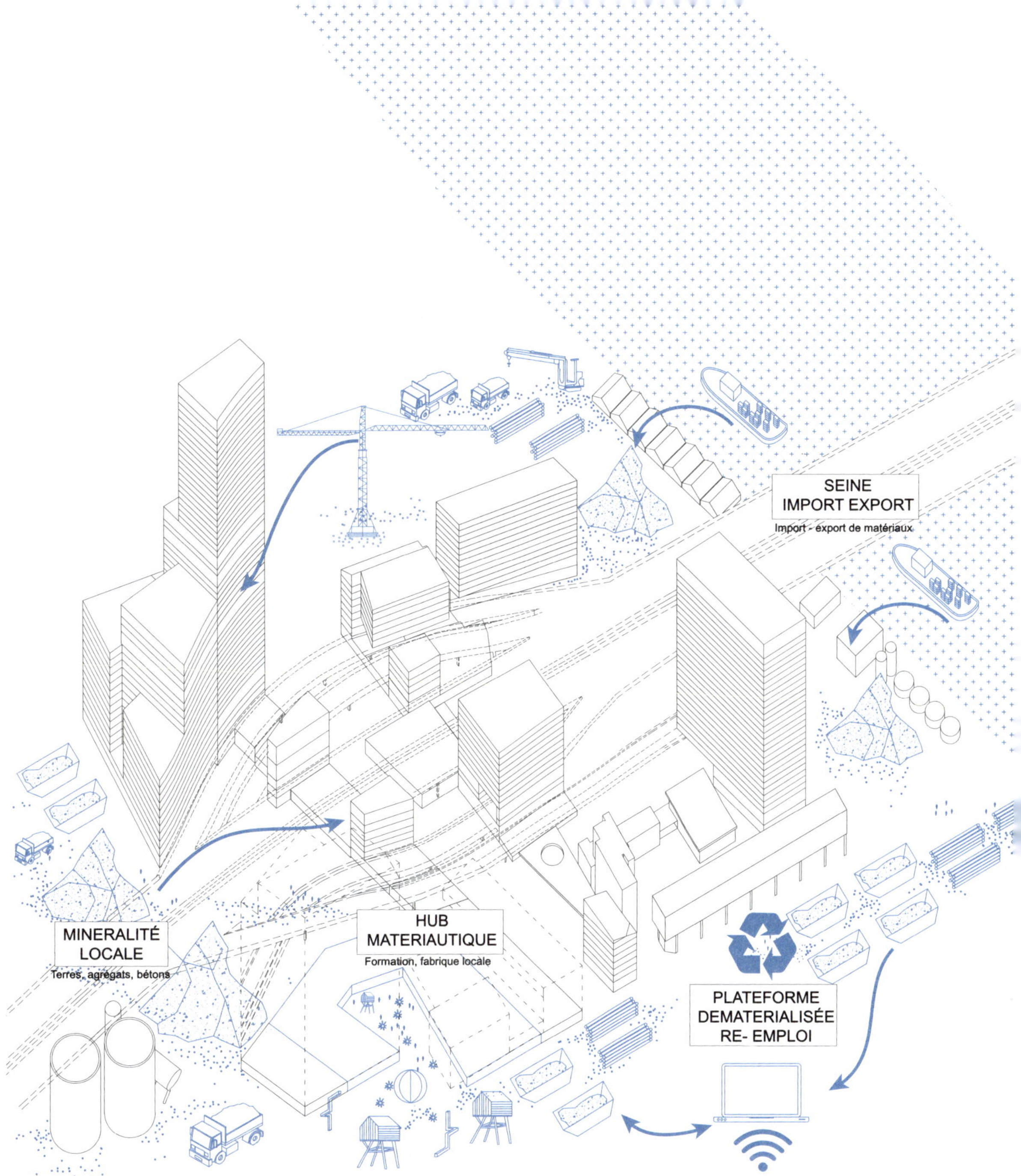

Circularity diagram

the framework of capable structures continues beyond the environment of the *boulevard périphérique* while offering adjustments in capacity. By occupying all the ground floors of the planned buildings, it constitutes a unified and open layer in direct contact with the urban space, while leaving the upper floors free to engage with it from time to time to hold collective activities, welcome the public, share programmes and create breathing spaces.

This approach to the city through precision and attention to existing resources is key to encouraging a mix of uses and populations. This quality, which originates in the Great Hall, extends through this new district. It is particularly visible in the tall building, which accommodates families, students and seniors, businesses and activities, following the organic nature of the roadway, aligning itself along the Paris-Ivry thoroughfare while letting itself be inhabited by the public.

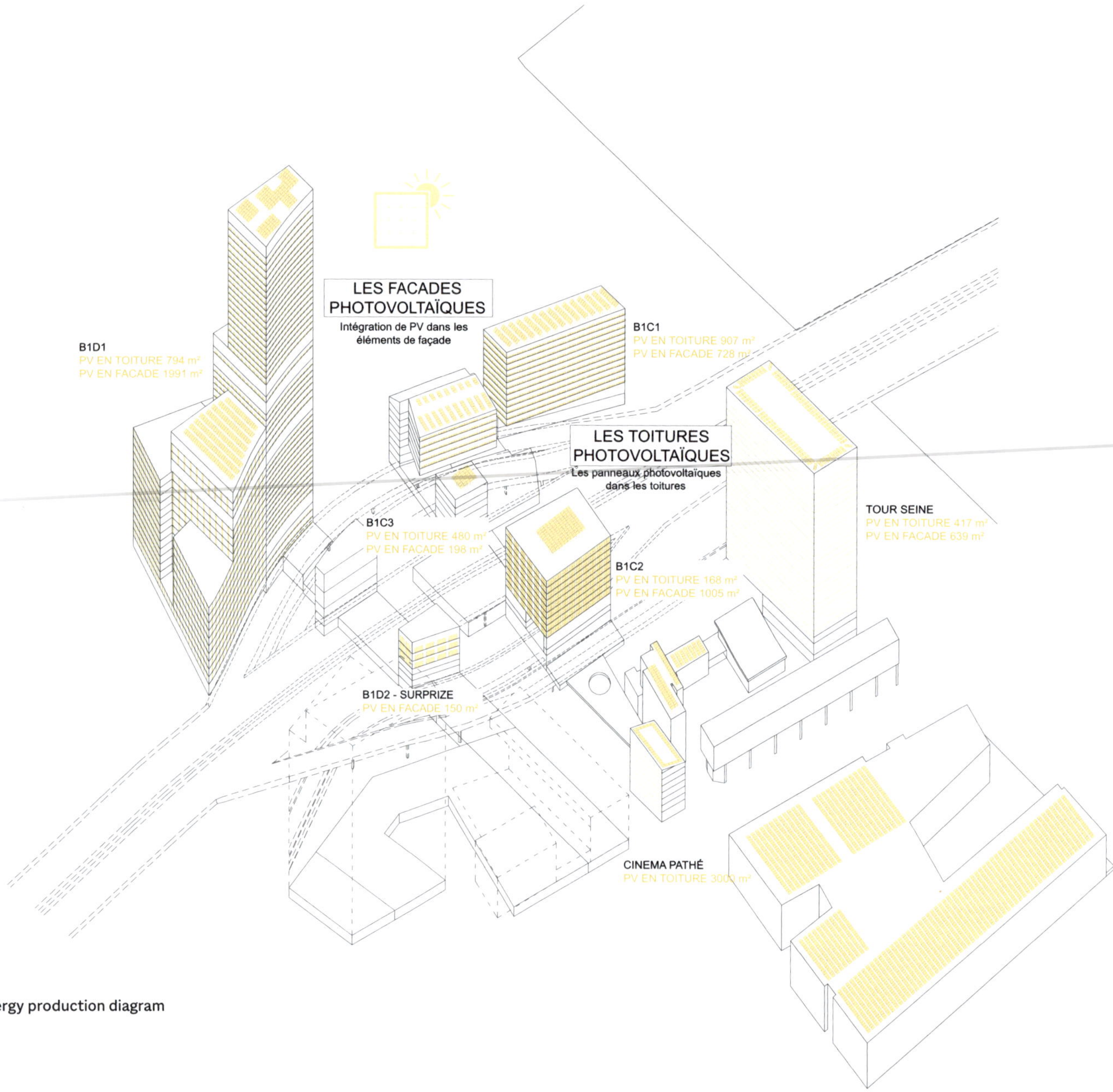

Energy production diagram

Echoing this very precise approach, the landscaping work will focus on the scale of proximity, detail, the garden and capable structures. Indeed, the greater landscape is already present: the banks of the Seine, the river, the elevated roadways. It is not a question of simulating it but of intervening in specific points and to measure, at ground level and above ground.
This project aims to question the dominant system of urban production. It is based on the disappearance of figures of power. By focusing on reversing a territory's weaknesses and working through interdependencies and the balancing of economic forces, any development situation can thus participate in an ecosystem of actions and a process of social transformation.

Karine Dana

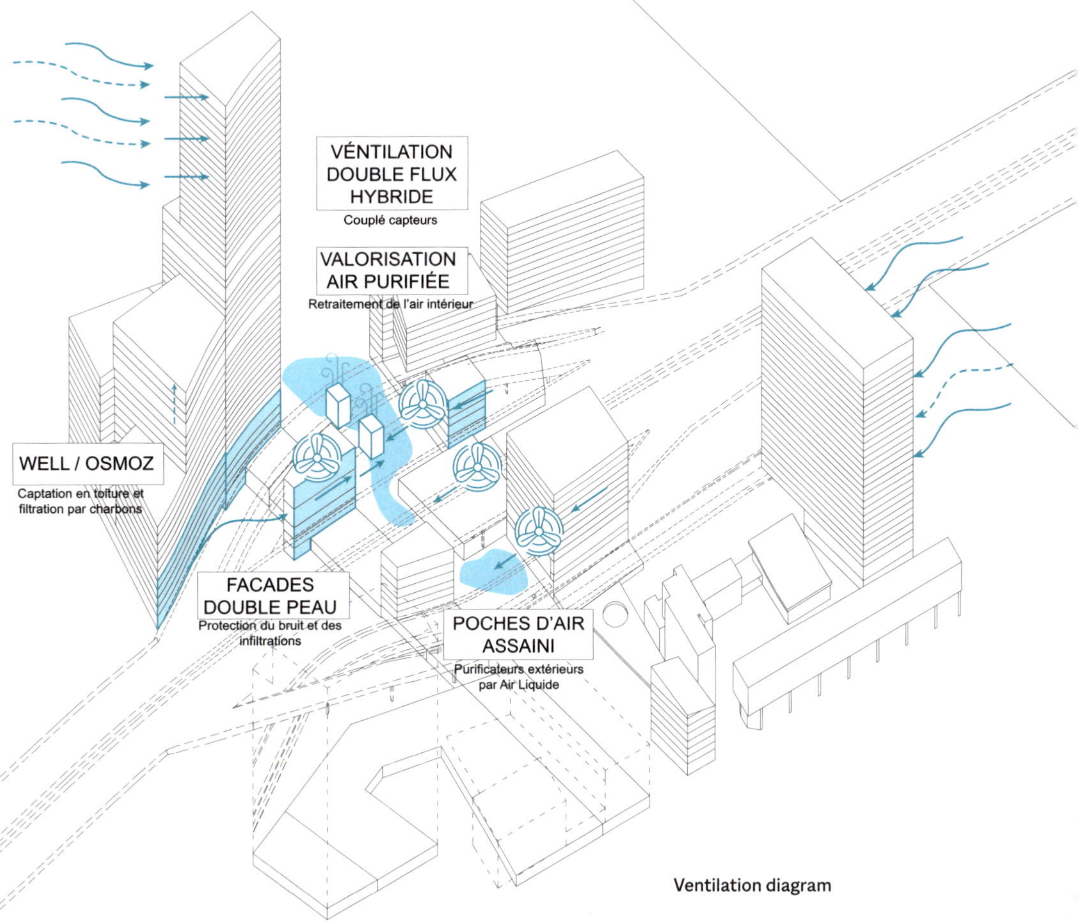

Ventilation diagram

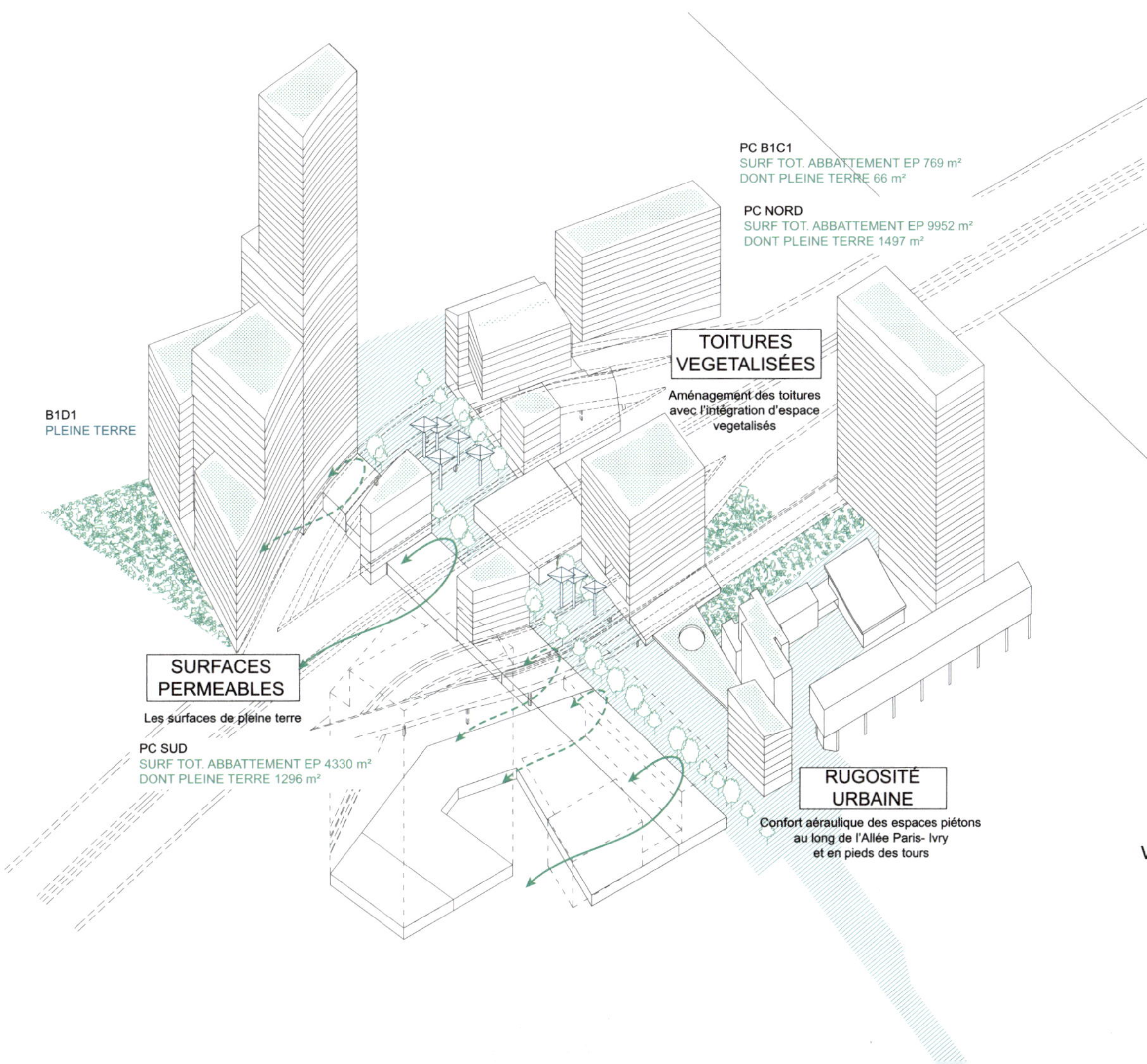

Vegetation diagram

BLF Disaster Center

Ghazir, Lebanon
2013–2020

This project demonstrates how programmatic specificity can become a means of expressing a political stance: the project for this disaster recovery site raises the fundamental question of space in times of war, but also of the relationship to the territory, which is itself the result of a state of war.

At the junction of two roads leading into the mountains, and just off the motorway leading to the sea, the BLF Disaster Centre emerges on a triangular plot.

In Lebanon, the Central Bank obliges all banking institutions to store private information in protected buildings that must be located in a territory with a low risk of attack. This indisputable logic, based on the need for security, has given rise to a secondary and equally pernicious form of warfare, but this time on landscapes and heritage. Thus, the village of Ghazir, like the entire Christian part of northern Beirut, has been gradually built up as a result of unchecked urban development linked to the exodus of populations during the war but also to the financial opportunities generated by the prevailing danger.

By inscribing this project in the territory in a manner that is both abstract and radical, Youssef Tohme adopts a critical attitude towards this impulsive and destructive urbanism of withdrawal caused by the war. Invoking the symbolism of the megalith, the architect seeks to create a pre-existence, an anteriority, in one of the most acculturated and devastated areas in the region around Beirut. "Even though the idea of the bunker can be frightening, in times of war it is a type of building that reassures people. You need to feel protected in your physical body. The envelope must express this overprotection. The legibility of this presence is all the more important given that the urban condition in which it is inserted is fundamentally sad", explains the architect who, with this project, inserts a strong, calm and perfectly enigmatic form into a site that is so full of chatter, characterised by buildings of all manner of height, blocked views of the sea, displays of neo-traditional materials and mountain slopes stripped of forest. The architectural curiosity that is the BLF Disaster Center imposes silence and gravity in this setting, through the imaginary of the fortress, of course, through its immediate relationship to public space, through the smooth skin of its concrete shell and its extremely precise implementation, but also through its discordant morphology that seems to invoke both sea and mountain. For the architect, building an "enigma", precisely in this location, is to question the history of the landscape.

This quest for anteriority corresponds to an interiority that also stems from the state of war. How does one experience space during wartime? And how does one keep working? "I tried to remember how I felt during the war in order to know what space I would like to be in. You have to understand that human relationships are disrupted when there is war. People feel a vital need to talk, to share their thoughts, to feel. There is no longer any hierarchy of space or function. Everyone lets themselves go because no one is in control. In times of war, you are one with others, you stand together, you shout, you scream. We are all connected by these common feelings", explains the architect.

Thus, at the junction of two roads leading into the mountains and just off the motorway leading to the sea, the BLF Disaster Center emerges on a triangular plot of land, surrounded by high-rise buildings, some of them unfinished and whose red tile and stone cladding suffice to qualify them as "integrated". Although relatively modest in terms of its footprint, it stands out strongly in this ruined territory. Easily accessible from the public space, it is made up of two concrete volumes with a glazed intermediary structure bridging the slight gap between them. The volumes give no indication of what they conceal: six basement levels in which client data is stored and protected. For its internal organisation, the architect arranged the workspaces around a large void. In this way, the heart of the main building is open to circulation, life, exchanges and proximity between people who can

View of the formwork used in the construction of the thin-wall concrete shells

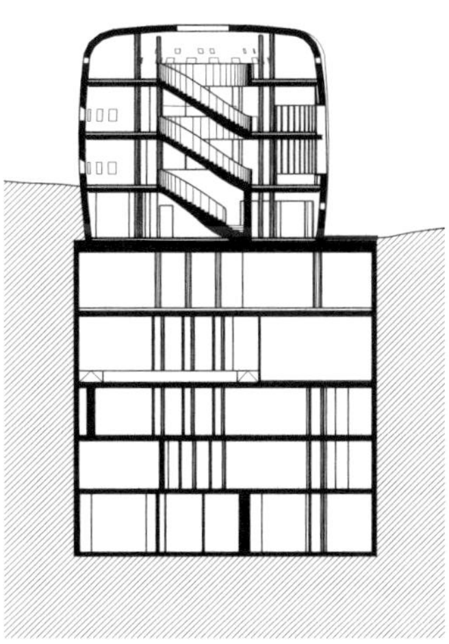

Cross-section

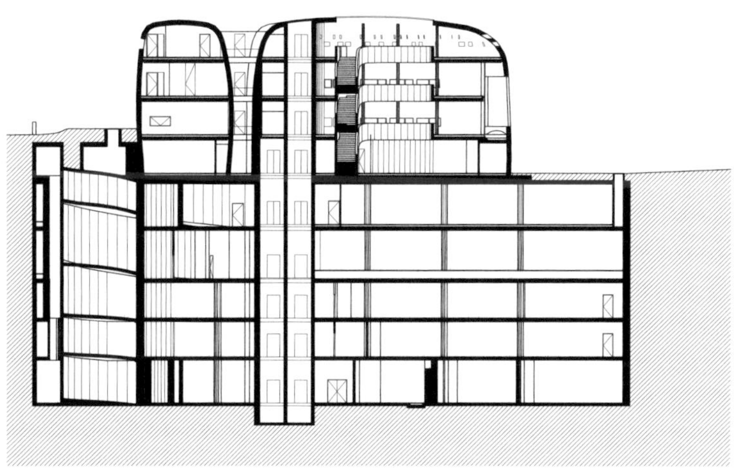

Longitudinal section

Left page: **The building is formed of two concrete volumes connected by a glazed intermediary structure; it protects six basement levels storing client data.**

Detail view of the concrete shells showing their very light and even colour

Left page: View of the construction site showing the complex process involved in building the concrete shell

see each other, speak to each other, reassure each other and do their work, in times of war as in normal times. The strengths of this argument convinced the client to accept a loss of surface area in exchange for gains in efficiency. This dilated space the architect likes to incorporate in his buildings, and which the client had greatly appreciated during their visit to Saint Joseph's University in Beirut, takes on a particular, vital meaning here.

Designed in close collaboration with engineer Nabil Hennaoui, as is the case for many of the office's operations, the BLF Disaster Center's structure constitutes its architecture. It is based on the principle of a thin concrete shell which, surprisingly, allows for openings. These openings, which are complex to integrate into a hollow, curved structure, are located at the foot and towards the top of the shell but also in the vertical part, forming important and disconcerting features of the building. They build the relationship to the territory, to the road, to the pavement and to public space. Their construction required a fine calculation of the load distribution so that the solid parts bear all the weight, sometimes reinforced by steel pillars. The interior spaces are separated into two distinct parts, namely the lower and upper sections of the building, which

The building is relatively modest in size, yet stands out in this area ruined by the destructive urbanism that followed the war.

The building is very easily accessible from public space.

Next page: **View of the central atrium and its concrete staircase and solid guardrail**

adhere to different constructional principles. The emerging part of the main entity, whose envelope works as a shell, is characterised by its large central void and its spiral concrete guardrail, which functions as a circulation ramp.
On the ground floor, a 90-centimetre transfer slab separates the space from the lower part of the building housing the data, whose grid of pillars offers great flexibility of use.
The execution and implementation of the main building shell was highly complex. The formwork had to be manufactured floor by floor using traditional techniques in order to achieve perfect flatness and surface continuity. To facilitate the construction of this formwork, a project in itself, the company created an almost full-scale model in its workshop. Thus, each layer cast on site overlaps exactly with the layer below.
The very light colour of the concrete and the uniformity of the surface sought by the architect added to the complexity of the construction, requiring the use of sand, gravel and cement extracted from the same site and stored in the same place.
This project, so intimately linked to the precision and delicacy of its implementation, uses concrete for its softness, its capacity to shape a world and to engage critically with a brutalised landscape.

Karine Dana

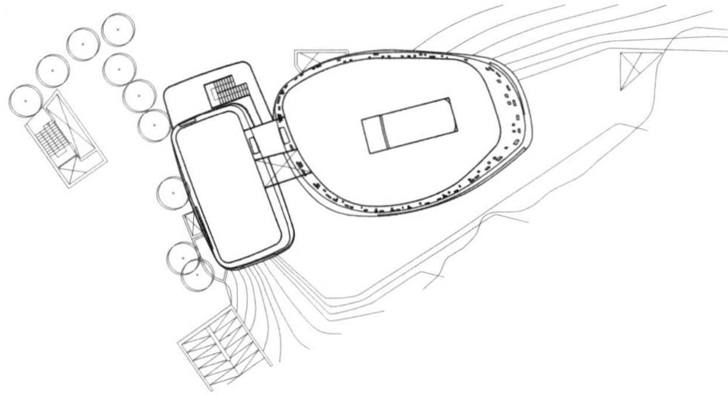

Roof plan

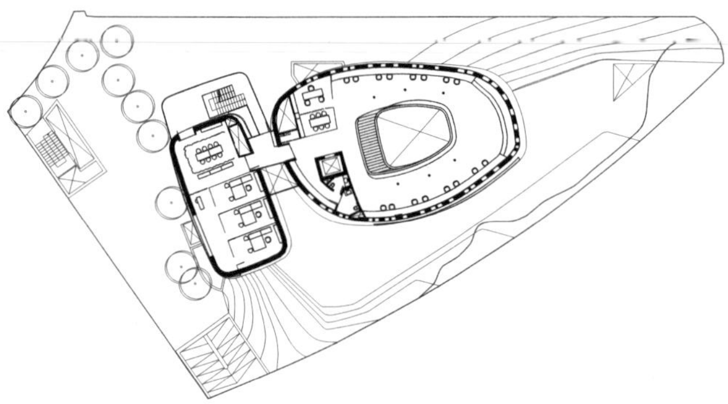

4th floor plan

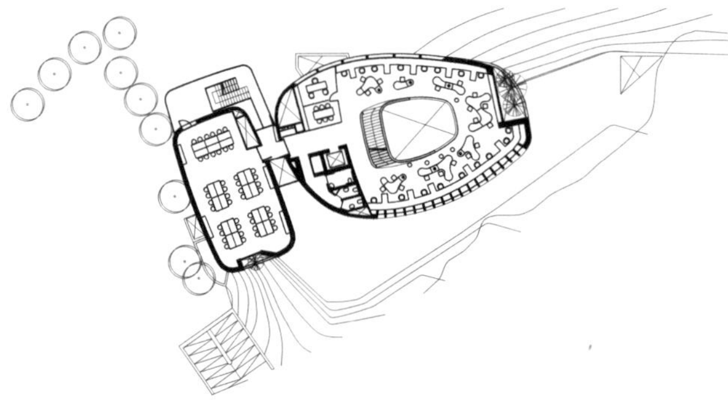

3rd floor plan

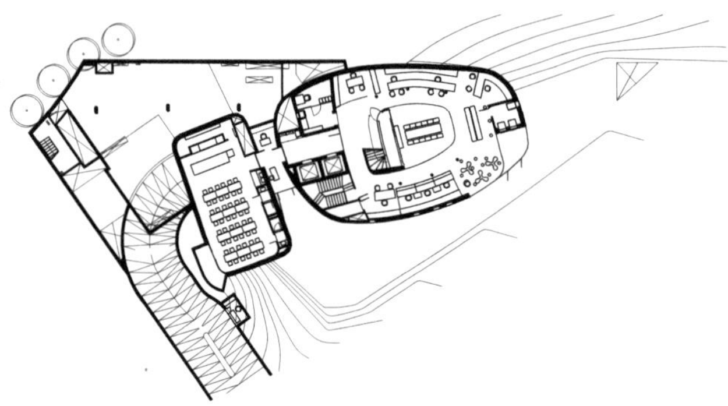

Ground floor plan

Right page: **View showing the organisation of the work spaces around the atrium, which is open to life, exchanges and proximity between people**

Kalani Resort

Halat, Lebanon
2012–2017

Byblos is a coastal city some fourty kilometres north of Beirut and one of the oldest continuously inhabited settlements on earth. From the third millennium BC until the Middle Ages, its port acquired great importance as a key hub for shipping papyrus. Numerous architectural monuments and ruins scattered across the city testify to its long history.

The composition of the individual pavilions and their sculptural effect

The Kalani Seascape Resort by Youssef Tohme Architects & Associates lies in the village of Halat, south of Byblos and thus in the direct proximity of one of Lebanon's most historic sites. The resort extends along a 220-metre stretch of the coastline and is separated into various individual buildings that together house thirteen hotel suites, a restaurant and an additional hotel area in simple, wood-slatted buildings and outbuildings. A long, narrow pool augments the private beach, which lies the other side of a shielding quarry-stone embankment and is reached by broad flights of steps leading down from the terrace. The two sizes of suites are housed in a cluster of individual structures at one end of the site. The suites impress through their striking forms: each structure is composed of three curved shells of in-situ cast concrete, their forms varying subtly across the group. Two curved shells enclose the sides of the structures while a third intersects at the back where the ancillary spaces such as the bathrooms are located. An access path runs along the rear, past the various services, and leads to the entrances. The two curved shells on either side direct one's view outwards towards the sea and rise upwards over the roof plane like the sails of boats.

Tohme's passion for experimenting with concrete and exploring the formal possibilities it presents is very evident in this project, and together with his specialist planners and contractors he has mastered the structural technicalities to create a unique architectural expression. The intention here was to allow the sail-like concrete shells to rest casually against one another, forming sheltered interiors between them. The resulting effect is one of great lightness and dramatic, eye-catching forms along the coastal road. Needless to say, the production of the formwork necessary to achieve this was a significant challenge.

Each suite has a gallery level reached via a free-standing spiral staircase that heightens the experience of the view outwards framed by the

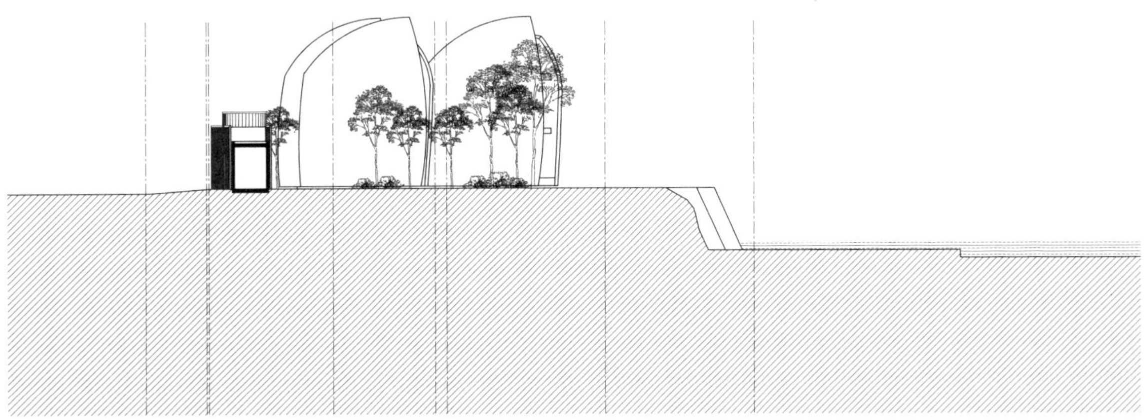

Cross-section through the complex

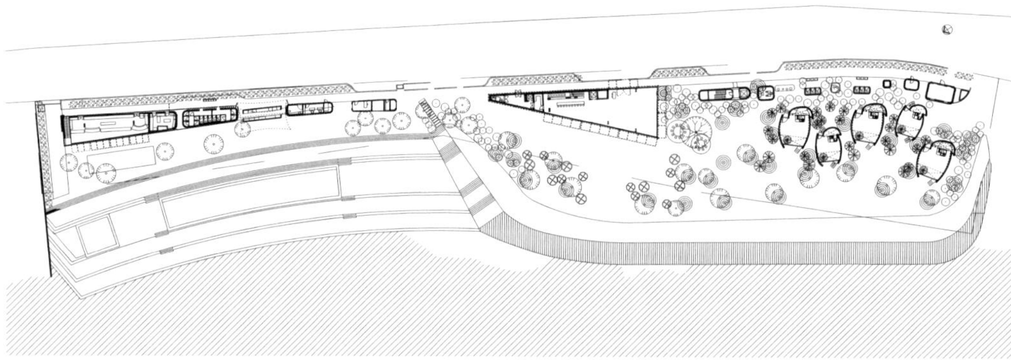

Roof view

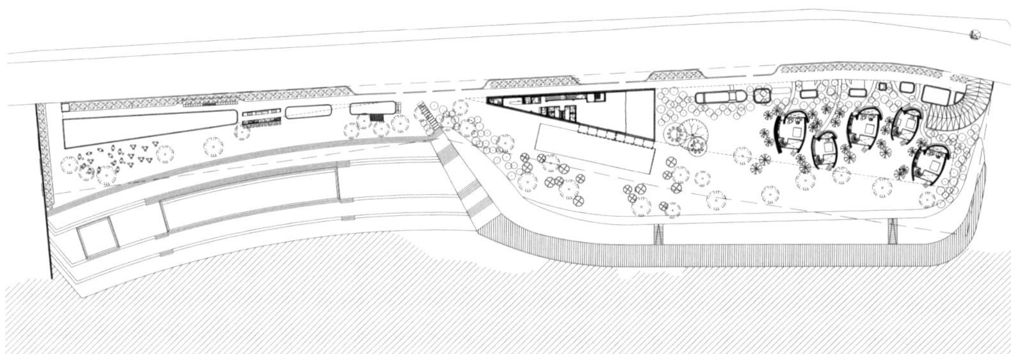

Upper floor

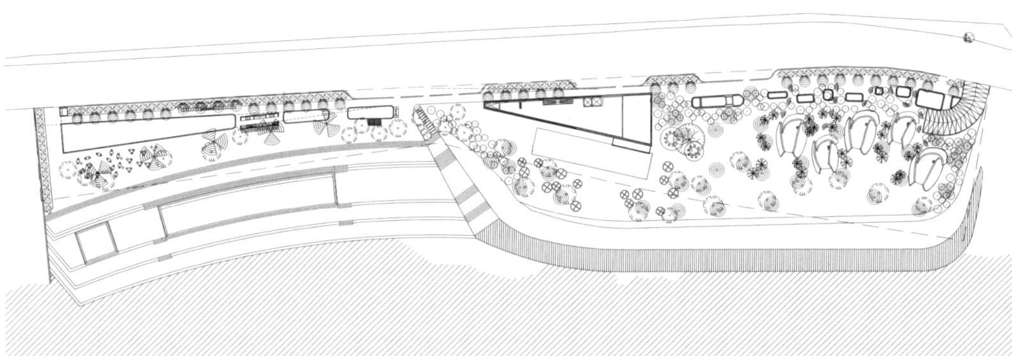

Ground floor

The bedroom pavilions blend into the coastal landscape.

A raised pool at one end of the complex overlooks the sea.

Each of the distinctive concrete shell pavilions has its own outdoor area.

Intricate formwork was constructed to cast the concrete shells on site.

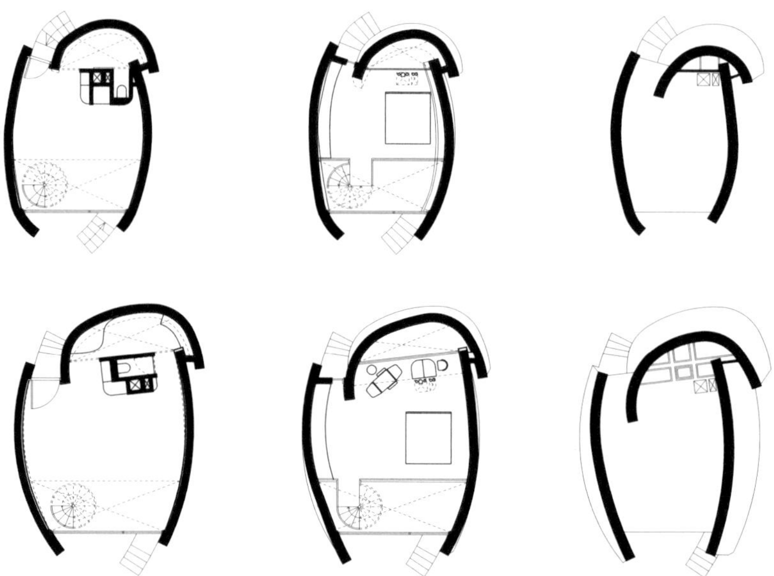

The different-sized pavilions are each composed of three shells.

irregular, curved organic forms of the walls. Slender profiles delineate the expansive glazing with its door onto the terrace for maximum transparency while palm trees provide a degree of shade from the sun. The architectural language and loose placement of the rounded buildings gives the impression that they are only tenuously anchored in place and could shift at any moment, like a small sailing regatta shifting and jostling for position—a quite delightful deception. The interiors of the suites, designed by studio 1millimetre, have been kept all-white and are sparsely furnished, not least due to the curved enclosing walls. Guests can enjoy a view of the sea from their bed on the upper gallery.

Sebastian Redecke

View into a pavilion. The bedroom is on the upper level.

Project Information

Villa SC
Akoura, Lebanon

Construction: 2010-2013
Type: Residence
Surface: 450 m^2
Architect: YTAA
Structural engineer: Esmat Elhachem
Consulting mechanical engineer: Roger Kazopoulo
Consulting electrical engineer: Gilbert Tambourgi
General contractor: LAYOUT contracting & consulting
Consulting interior architect: Rania Sabbagh

Villa T
Kornet Chehouane, Lebanon

Construction: 2008-2014
Type: Residence
Surface: 2,500 m^2
Architect: Youssef Tohme
Structural engineer: Nabil G.Hennaoui
Consulting mechanical engineer: Roger Kazopoulo
Consulting electrical engineer: Gilbert Tambourgi
General contractor: Ent. Hakime
Finishing contractor: Khater Contracting Group
Consulting interior architect: Rania Sabbagh

USJ Innovation, Economy and Sports Campus
Beirut, Lebanon

Construction: 2004-2012
Type: Campus
Surface: 60,000 m^2
Architect: Youssef Tohme and 109 Architectes
Consulting structural engineer: Rodolphe Matar
Consulting mechanical engineer: Ibrahim Mounayar
Consulting electrical engineer: Georges Chamoun
Main contractor: Ent. Hakime

Ilot sur le Parc
Marseille, France

Competition

Construction: 2019-ongoing
Type: Mixed use
Surface: 6,750 m^2
Architect: YTAA
Client: Melt, Altarea Cogedim
Project manager: L'Effet Urbain
Consulting environmental engineer: Sinteo
Consulting mechanical engineer: Sigma Ingénierie
Consulting electrical engineer: Sigma Ingénierie
Project and cost management: VPEAS
Consulting landscape architect: Atelier Der Sahakian

A599 Apartment Building
Ashrafieh, Beirut, Lebanon

Construction: 2013-2019
Type: Residence
Surface: 9,000 m^2
Architect: YTAA
Client: Al-Mawarid Real Estate
Consulting structural engineer: Nabil G. Hennaoui
Consulting electrical and mechanical engineer: Wissam Tawil & Associates/MEP engineers
Project manager: Ayman Sanyoura Architecture & Management
Main contractor: Mouawad-Edde

MARe—Muzeul de ArtăRecentă
Bucharest, Romania

Construction: 2013-2018
Type: Culture
Surface: 1,580 m^2
Architect: YTAA
Client: Roger Akoury
Consulting structural engineer: Ductil Tech.
Consulting electrical engineer: Wissam Tawil & Associates
Consulting mechanical engineer: Wissam Tawil & Associates
Project manager: Walid Zaarour
Main contractor: Colina Development
Consulting landscape architect: Ana Marti-Baron

Villa M
Kornet Chehouane, Lebanon

Construction: 2015-2018
Type: Residence
Surface: 1,800 m^2
Architect: Youssef Tohme
Client: Private
Consulting structural engineer: Nabil G. Hennaoui
Consulting mechanical engineer: Roger Kazopoulo
Consulting electrical engineer: Gilbert Tambourgi
Main contractor: Ent. Hakime

Villa VR
Ajaltoun, Lebanon

Construction: 2011-2016
Type: Residence
Surface: 1,800 m^2
Architect: YTAA
Client: Private
Consulting structural engineer: Nabil G. Hennaoui S.A.L.
Consulting electrical engineer: Gilbert Tambourgi
Consulting mechanical engineer: Roger Kazopoulo
Project manager: Charles E. Maroun Consult
Main contractor: Ent. Hakime

Brazza District
Bordeaux, France

Construction: 2012–2030
Type: Urban Planning
Surface: 600,000 m²
Architect: YTAA
Client: Bordeaux Métropole
Project manager: Mairie de Bordeaux
Consulting mechanical engineer: INGEROP
Consulting electrical engineer: INGEROP
Consulting landscape architect:
Michel Desvigne Paysagiste

Quartier Bruneseau
Paris, France

Construction: 2018–ongoing
Type: Mixed use
Surface: 100,000 m²
Architects team: YTAA, Hardel Le Bihan Architectes, Adjaye Associates, Buzzo Spinelli
Landscape: Bassinet Turquain Paysage
Client: Les Nouveaux Constructeurs/AG Real Estate France/ Icade/Nexity
Consulting environmental engineer: Elioth, CDC Biodiversité
Consulting structural, safety and acoustic engineer:
Egis Bâtiment
Consulting electrical and mechanical engineer: iLAB
Wood construction: Mathis
Mobility consultant : Sareco

BLF Disaster Center
Ghazir, Lebanon

Construction: 2013–2020
Type: Commerce
Surface: 7,850 m²
Architect: YTAA
Client: Private
Project manager: Charles E. Maroun Consult
Structural engineer: Nabil G. Hennaoui S.A.L.
Consulting electrical and mechanical engineer: Barbanel
Main contractor: Ent. Hakime

Kalani Resort
Halat, Lebanon

Construction: 2012–2017
Type: Resort
Surface: 5,000 m²
Architect: YTAA
Client: Lazy Daze
Consulting structural engineer: Nabil Hennaoui
Consulting mechanical engineer: Wissam Tawil & Associates/ MEP engineers
Consulting electrical engineer: Wissam Tawil & Associates/ MEP engineers
Project and cost management: Charles E. Maroun Consult
General finishing contractor: Khater Contracting Group
Consulting landscape architect: Bas Smets
Consulting interior architect: 1millimetre

Conversation entre Youssef Tohme et Karine Dana

J'aimerais que l'on mène ensemble une conversation qui « transforme »... Le point de départ sera le plus important car ces échanges ne vont pas vraiment se terminer.
Pouvez-vous nous raconter comment les choses commencent ?

En tant qu'architecte, je suis à la recherche d'une relation au monde à la fois très précise et indéterminée : je voudrais me sentir à l'intérieur d'un lieu comme dans le désert, dans la mer ou au-dessus des nuages - dans 360 degrés de vide chargé d'espace. Cette quête initiale traverse tous nos projets. J'aspire inlassablement à construire un état sans référence, un état simultané d'ancrage et de suspension de soi auquel on ne peut qu'appartenir. Il s'agit d'une condition d'absolue solitude et tout en même temps d'attache, de lien profond au milieu.
Ces situations d'indétermination et d'imprévisibilité, d'absence de limite me semblent nécessaires au relâchement humain. Alors seulement, on peut traverser l'espace et être traversé par lui et, peut-être, vidé de ses angoisses. Ce rattachement très fort, ce sentiment d'être là, en même temps que le monde, dans son présent, dans son épaisseur, dans sa masse et son mouvement, est préliminaire à tout ce que je veux concevoir et construire. Je veux créer des lieux de perte d'orientation qui apportent des vertiges et du silence, des lieux en « mode avion » !
Ainsi, pour chacun des projets de l'agence, nous essayons toujours de créer une dynamique et son contraire. C'est une façon de mettre l'humain dans un état de lâcher-prise, extraordinairement physique et présent. Je cherche en l'homme cet état de porosité, d'éveil et d'ivresse par l'espace, semblable à celui où l'amour ou un baiser sont capables de nous plonger. Toute notre architecture relève de cette quête de relation : trouver le point de rencontre immensément fragile entre l'intime et le collectif. Le collectif n'est pas le nombre, le collectif est le milieu. Cette recherche obsessionnelle est déterminante dans mon travail, elle explique toutes mes tentations. C'est une recherche de naïveté. Un état de rêve, de liberté ouverte que j'aimerais toucher à travers chacun de mes projets.

Quelles expériences spatiales vous ont le plus marqué ?

Mon enfance a été imprégnée d'expériences spatiales fondamentales. Celle de la mer, avant tout : le seul paysage dans lequel on peut vraiment entrer. Être dans la mer, toucher sa douceur, être entouré par les effets du vent sur l'eau, en faire ainsi partie - cette situation procure une force incroyable liée à une privation totale de repère. La sensation d'être connecté à plus grand que soi et en même temps d'être dans cet intérieur est si particulière... Elle tient notamment à l'absence de projection et de représentation possibles. Et cela m'émeut beaucoup.
La mer m'a appris ce que signifient une ambiance et un ressenti. Quand je veux m'imprégner d'une architecture et la comprendre, je la regarde en fronçant les sourcils et en plissant les yeux, comme si j'étais sous l'eau, sans masque, les yeux ouverts malgré tout. C'est en ouvrant les yeux que j'ai appris ce qu'était la mer. Il ne s'agit pas simplement de la voir mais d'entrer dedans, que la peau et les pupilles, en même temps, en sentent le contact et le vivent. C'est une sensation très physique mais qui renvoie également à un échappement total. C'est peut-être précisément cela la définition d'une ambiance. La mer m'a enseigné l'architecture. Elle nous enseigne que même quand tout est bloqué, on peut toujours échapper.
Quand j'ai commencé mes études d'architecture, j'ai analysé les villes portuaires ou maritimes. Pourquoi se sent-on si bien dans ces villes ? J'ai compris que dans une ville, la seule présence de la mer génère du lien social et nous détache de tout. La mer a ce pouvoir de prendre le dessus sur le bâti, sur l'espace public et les routes, sur les mots, sur le bruit. La mer nous apprend le silence et l'abstraction. J'ai compris aussi que la mer pouvait effacer les limites de tout ordre établi, de tout pouvoir en place. On l'invite, elle vient chez nous et elle nous remplit, elle se répand même si on n'a qu'un petit espace. La mer produit de l'effacement et de l'échappement car elle nous décentre. Il est très important de se dire aujourd'hui que l'humain n'est plus le centre.
La mer a eu un impact énorme sur moi et sur ma façon de travailler, du plus petit au plus grand des espaces, qu'ils soient individuels ou publics. Je perçois la même chose dans le désert ou sur un toit, c'est une puissance qu'on habite. Voilà le début de l'histoire : fabriquer des paysages pénétrables dans lesquels on habite, on descend, on flotte, on nage, on échange, on se tait.
Ces souvenirs d'espace ne me quittent jamais et guident chacun des projets. Ainsi, je cherche toujours

à ramener le programme, l'usage, la structure, à cette idée précise de l'étendue qui invite, qui intègre et se laisse habiter. Cela veut dire que je ne veux pas cerner mais au contraire ouvrir, libérer les espaces. Je ne travaille jamais sur des paramètres qui réduisent ou renvoient à des échelles de référence ou à des standards. Ainsi, une maison n'est jamais vraiment une maison, c'est un lieu qui nous remet à notre place. Et cela implique de perdre ses repères. C'est fondamental. Les plus grandes expériences spatiales que l'on puisse connaître se produisent quand il n'y a absolument plus aucun jalon, quand on est soi-même vide, vidé, totalement disponible pour échanger avec son milieu - d'égal à égal.

Je me souviens aussi avoir traversé en bateau des paysages où le flanc des montagnes venait plonger dans la mer. C'était très perturbant. La montagne est associée pour moi à l'idée de *layers*, de succession de séquences. Ainsi, plus j'avançais sur l'eau, plus le paysage semblait reculer. À chaque fois que je me rapprochais d'une couche, une autre apparaissait.

En architecture, construire l'espace à partir de *layers* permet de perturber la réalité. Cela nous introduit dans un état de rêve, là encore dénué de toute référence : un état de totale abstraction et où seul joue l'espace. Quand, à l'agence, nous avons conçu la Villa T et la Villa SC, les premières maisons que nous avons construites au Liban, c'est précisément la recherche de ces conditions qui a guidé les projets. Nous n'avons pas cherché à dessiner mais à effacer. Nous n'avons pas cherché à représenter ni à rassurer mais à brouiller. Nous n'avons pas cherché à clore ou à cerner mais à ouvrir et soustraire les façades. La Villa SC est un simple muret accueillant un trou. Dans les deux projets, l'idée de maison disparaît.

Dans un pays comme le Liban, où la notion de représentation est si forte et si politique, comment vous positionnez-vous en tant qu'architecte ?

Renoncer à exprimer une représentation ou une appartenance, quand on vit au Liban, renvoie à une forme d'engagement. Je travaille dans un pays où les questions d'identités si multiples et fragmentées sont tellement ancrées et rattachées à la guerre… L'expérience de ces fractures, de ces limites, de ces conventions et de ces replis est encore très fraîche en moi. Je me bats, en tant qu'architecte et avec les armes de l'architecte, contre ces idées-là.

Je me suis longtemps questionné sur les concepts de représentation, tellement forts et importants au Liban. Cette question, sous-jacente à toute action, ne peut pas être évacuée facilement. Elle a donc un impact sur le territoire. C'est pourquoi je lutte pour casser le poids de l'image car ce poids limite, enferme, catégorise, assimile. En cela, je cherche toujours à effacer les références et je ne veux pas représenter d'illusion de départ. Seules m'intéressent les situations d'échange. Je cherche à construire un lien commun.

En tant qu'architecte, je crois intimement en la douceur. Je pense que les choses ne sont pas toujours des conflits. Je défends une vision romantique du monde. Cela signifie que je suis idéaliste et résistant. Je crois qu'il peut y avoir de la délicatesse partout. La ville de Beyrouth n'est pas réductible à une morphologie agressive, il y a aussi beaucoup de douceur dans la ville, un climat, une géographie, des contacts faciles, une intensité et une chaleur. J'essaie d'intérioriser ces conditions intimes dans mes projets. Cette douceur est porteuse d'une ambiance spécifique. C'est cela qui nous rattache à Beyrouth, une certaine magie, une résilience qui permet à toutes les limites de se déplacer. C'est ce qu'il faut garder.

Comment ce concept de douceur est-il abordé dans vos projets ?

Dans chacun de nos projets, nous essayons de construire cette intériorité ambivalente faite d'ancrage et de détachement. C'est pour moi la définition même de la condition libanaise : un état de contradiction permanente, à la fois tendu et doux. Je ne veux rien faire du chaos, je ne veux pas m'en servir. Je défends le concept de douceur en architecture. Il s'agit pour moi d'un acte d'engagement. La douceur vient toujours en même temps qu'une certaine brutalité et en réaction à celle-ci.

Quand je pose un projet sur un territoire, je cherche toujours à calmer la situation par l'architecture, à travers la matière, l'ambiance, l'implantation. Dans la situation d'extrême confusion où nous nous trouvons, la douceur est une réponse forte. Elle n'agit pas comme une image ou une référence, mais comme un silence, une brume, un courant d'air, comme la mer.

Cette opposition m'intéresse, je pense qu'elle est porteuse d'une réelle intensité. Les choses sont dures mais on peut les voir avec un autre regard. Je refuse l'exclusivité et l'unicité du regard. Même quand une situation est difficile, on peut toujours faire infuser autre chose. Il y a une réelle puissance de la douceur comme refus de l'agressivité et du déterminisme. Être

dans un état de douceur permet de mieux écouter le territoire. C'est pour moi une nécessité.
À travers nos projets, nous essayons toujours d'amener un regard qui adoucit, résultant du fait que nous sommes attentifs et alertes. La douceur vient par l'observation. Quand le soleil accroche le béton et qu'il entre à l'intérieur d'un espace, tout à coup survient la possibilité d'une douceur.
Être doux c'est parvenir à être compréhensif, c'est aussi admettre notre vulnérabilité. C'est un choix, une position. Il y a du charnel et du spirituel dans la douceur. Il y a du tactile lié à la main, à la bouche, à la peau. Il y a toujours aussi la proximité possible de l'abîme, du brutal, de l'opaque. Toutes les situations auxquelles doit faire face l'architecte sont des situations inquiétées. Être doux induit une volonté de comprendre, de se rapprocher, de faire confiance, de stabiliser. Ce n'est pas une faiblesse mais une puissance. C'est une affaire de tact et de non-résignation. Travailler, exercer la douceur signifie prendre conscience de la complexité et sans doute aussi continuer d'appartenir à l'enfance.
La douceur est une philosophie du regard, une philosophie de la présence. Elle donne les clés d'une phénoménologie de l'espace. En tant qu'architecte, je rattache cela à une approche non matérialiste de l'espace qui porte sur la lumière, l'air, le silence, le vide, les rebonds du soleil. Le concept de douceur permet de parler d'architecture avec des moyens immatériels, et c'est très fort. Il amène ainsi la question du fondamental et de la primitivité d'un contexte.
Le concept de douceur exprime un refus de parler, une résistance contre l'état du monde, contre ce langage-là. C'est une arme pour se battre en architecte, au Liban ou ailleurs, contre la finitude, contre toutes les formes de fermeture, et contre les certitudes.
La douceur renvoie à l'idée d'intériorité ouverte. C'est le contraire d'une bulle. En tant qu'architecte, je ne cherche pas à fabriquer des mondes mais à constamment me demander comment laisser entrer le monde extérieur, jusqu'où m'ouvrir à lui, et comment échanger. Par la douceur, justement, on reste au monde, on lui répond, on garde cette porosité. C'est capital.
Par les projets, je ne veux pas créer des situations d'isolement ni de ponctuelles illusions de résolution. Dans la Villa T, j'amène de la douceur car le contexte me questionne. J'y réponds en m'ouvrant le plus possible jusqu'à rendre illisible l'image même de la maison.

La douceur, telle que vous l'envisagez, semble constituer une nouvelle forme de radicalité. Elle correspond à la fois à un point de vue et à un nouveau commencement…

Oui, c'est une forme de radicalité, au même titre que la nuance et le brouillage. La radicalité en architecture, longtemps fondée sur l'idée de rupture, se cherche d'autres vêtements aujourd'hui. On a longtemps cru en architecture à une radicalité de force, de guerre, de coup d'éclat. Au nom de cette radicalité de scission, on a beaucoup opposé les personnes entre elles. Il est grand temps d'explorer d'autres voies, plus subtiles, plus « nuageuses ». L'attitude de douceur, si elle peut se revendiquer dans l'architecture, s'exprime en amont des projets. C'est une manière habile de négocier, d'inciter à l'échange, d'exclure le conflit. S'il n'y a plus de rapport de force, cela devient intéressant et favorable aux architectes. Le concept de douceur en architecture est finalement très déstabilisant.
Au Liban, où le silence a très peu de place, où chaque vide doit être comblé, amener cette vision de douceur est particulièrement important. C'est un acte politique. Cela permet de faire taire, non seulement les voix et les engins, mais aussi les signes, les connotations, les représentations. En cela la douceur est une bonne compagne de l'abstraction ainsi qu'un précieux outil de projet.
Dans notre travail de requalification du site de Brazza à Bordeaux, nous avons développé l'idée du silence dans l'espace public. Les « pensoirs silencieux » de Nietzche nous ont inspiré les lanières de paysage qui traversent cet ancien site industriel du nord au sud. « Il faudra reconnaître un jour – et je pense qu'il viendra vite – que ce qui manque le plus à nos villes, ce sont des "pensoirs" silencieux et spacieux, de vastes endroits, avec de hautes longues galeries pour le mauvais temps et le grand soleil, où le bruit des voitures et les cris des marchands ne pénètrent pas, et où le tact interdise même aux prêtres de prier à haute voix : des bâtiments et des promenades qui expriment par leur ensemble la sublimité de la méditation et de l'isolement », écrit Nietzsche en 1882 dans *Le Gai Savoir*.
Je pense fondamentalement que la douceur peut amener l'échange. Elle permet de créer un espace pour le silence dans un champ de parole, et le temps de la compréhension. Elle conduit à se demander quoi faire pour qu'un lien existe et se crée. Elle implique l'autre, et donc le milieu. Si l'échange ne se produit pas, la douceur ne sert à rien : être doux uniquement pour soi ne me semble pas vraiment utile.

Dans les projets que nous développons, nous essayons toujours d'entrer en dialogue avec ce qui dysfonctionne pour, justement, structurer par la douceur. Nous ne cherchons pas à disparaître dans la partie du contexte existant qui ne fonctionne pas, ni à nous en isoler, ni à l'exhiber.
Cette nécessité de penser ainsi l'espace, en dehors des signes et des bruits, l'espace du silence, me vient du pouvoir de la mer. Je pense que le silence n'est autre que le présent. C'est peut-être pour cela qu'il fait si peur : au même titre qu'un imprévu ou un accident qui s'immisce dans une journée, il nous ramène subitement au réel. Sans silence, je pense qu'on ne peut pas évoluer. Il nous permet d'écouter, d'apprendre le présent et, en tant qu'architecte, c'est fondamental. Si on n'écoute pas le présent, c'est-à-dire le milieu, si on ne se rend pas compte de cette chance de sentir le réel, la douceur, le soleil, les choses vitales, je ne sais pas comment ni dans quoi on peut faire vivre les gens.

Comment s'intéresser aujourd'hui à l'espace et à ce qui le charge ?

L'espace serait cette énergie qui reste en nous après avoir traversé un lieu et que nous laissons en le traversant. Il naît d'une fonction primaire d'échange et de respiration entre le vivant et le monde. Il s'agit là d'un espace « terrestre », au sens où Bruno Latour peut en parler. Cette dimension du terrestre dans la pensée de l'espace rend les choses implacables.
Il y a peut-être une continuité entre la « nature » et notre intériorité qui n'a plus été respectée au moment du passage à la modernité. Nous nous sommes mis à l'écart. Nous avons brisé l'échange. Mais alors, par quoi sommes-nous traversés ? Notre espace ne se serait-il pas fondamentalement appauvri, comme notre capacité à parler des choses qui nous traversent ? C'est pourquoi je pense qu'il faut réapprendre à lâcher prise, réapprendre à perdre, à se laisser surprendre, à ne pas maîtriser le monde. C'est alors que l'on peut échapper, basculer, se libérer. Il faut réapprendre à accepter le risque, le vertige pour échapper, peut-être, à nos angoisses. En tant qu'architecte, je cherche à construire des dispositifs d'échappement, de libération, d'imagination pour l'habitant. En cela, l'architecture peut nous aider à guérir un peu.
En architecture, les dispositifs de lâcher-prise se concrétisent, paradoxalement, par cette idée d'être en prise sur le monde, le présent. L'architecture, en ce sens, a peut-être le pouvoir de calmer les angoisses collectives, qu'il s'agisse d'habitat individuel ou d'espace public, car elle peut dégager les obstacles et les contraintes autour de nous. Je pense que fondamentalement, l'architecture a le pouvoir de nous ramener à la vie. Sa concrétude, les mouvements qu'elle active, ce qu'elle touche en nous, contribuent à nous rattacher à la réalité du présent.
Qu'est ce qui fait qu'un espace rend libre ? Qu'on lâche prise quand on est quelque part ou que l'on n'y parvient pas ? Comment le fait d'être dedans nous permet-il d'être ailleurs ? Si l'on met l'habitant en situation de présent, d'inattendu, d'équivoque, d'illimité, il a peut-être une chance d'accéder à ces états de grâce par l'architecture. Pour se laisser aller, il faut accepter de ne rien maîtriser. L'architecture contribue à ce renoncement. Et tant qu'on pense qu'on peut maîtriser, on est maintenu dans l'angoisse… Se laisser aller, c'est se laisser traverser par l'espace. Ainsi, l'architecture permet de toucher les questions profondes de l'être-au-monde.

Cette question de l'imprévisible comme élément constitutif du projet a toujours été prédominante dans votre travail…

Depuis longtemps, j'ai compris que l'on ne maîtrisait rien, jamais. Cela paraît évident sur toute la planète aujourd'hui ! Ce postulat que j'ai en tête depuis l'enfance oblige à s'ouvrir au monde et à saisir toutes les contraintes comme une opportunité de conception. Cela oblige à faire confiance, à faire sans cesse le deuil de ce qu'on attend, à croire et concevoir aussi avec le hasard. J'agis ainsi en architecte.
Nous essayons de faire vivre cette notion d'imprévisible à travers nos projets. C'est une manière de travailler très en amont avec le site, le programme, les clients mais aussi avec l'espace. Je laisse toujours une marge et un espace entre les choses. C'est ma manière d'accueillir l'imprévu, de susciter sa visite et d'anticiper ses inconvenances. Cette marge n'est pas un reliquat. C'est un espace à part entière qui porte la condition de potentiels nouveaux. La plus-value d'un projet, sa part de réussite, d'inexplicable plaisir tient, selon nous, à cet imprévu en lui, qui permet d'embarquer l'habitant dans une histoire parallèle. Il crée la capacité et la potentialité du projet, au-delà de ce qui est déjà là. Alors les habitants, les acteurs du projet se saisissent ou non de cet espace intermédiaire et indéfini. Cela ne dépend plus de nous, mais le potentiel est là. Chaque projet a ainsi sa part de hasard, comme

autant d'ouvertures possibles, de nouveaux regards et de re-questionnements.
Il est très difficile d'intégrer et de faire accepter la notion d'imprévisible dans les conditions de projet, tout comme la notion d'espace indéterminé. C'est absolument contraire au fonctionnement de notre économie moderne et de notre rapport au monde. Or, je pense que ce sont les clés d'un bon projet. Ce saut, cet espace m'intéresse. Il faut comprendre que l'on peut trouver de l'ailleurs, de l'autre, dans l'imprévu et qu'il s'agit là d'un enseignement pour nous tous.

Le compositeur John Cage a écrit : « La structure sans la vie est morte. Mais la vie sans la structure est in-visible. La vie pure s'exprime dans et à travers la structure. » Que sert la structure dans vos projets ?

Cette réflexion me touche beaucoup ! La question de la structure rejoint selon moi la question de la vie et de l'incertitude.
L'épidémie que nous connaissons actuellement nous conduit précisément à expérimenter l'incertitude, un sentiment que la France n'a pas connu depuis la Seconde Guerre mondiale. Jusqu'à présent, on s'est permis de penser que l'on s'approchait d'un risque d'instabilité proche de zéro, tel un acquis construit et gagné au fil du temps en matière de diplomatie, de garanties, de santé publique, de prévention... Cette croyance m'a toujours choqué. J'ai toujours trouvé invraisemblable que l'on puisse être sûr de quoi que ce soit. Depuis mon enfance, je sais que rien n'est vraiment assuré, et qu'un équilibre est nécessairement instable et mouvant. C'est une pensée partagée par chacun au Liban où, évidemment, aucune structure ne rassure. Cette conscience fondamentale du mouvement et du changement est ancrée dans nos esprits. On sait que l'on ne peut jamais s'appuyer ni se reposer sur rien et que l'on doit trouver les assemblages qui permettent à toutes les interdépendances de fonctionner ensemble et de se soutenir. Cela implique que tous les éléments constitutifs d'une société humaine participent.
On peut se demander comment un pays comme le Liban fait pour tenir : il tient par la force et l'énergie qui existent par les personnes et entre les personnes. Il n'y a pas vraiment de structure. Il n'y a que la vie humaine, l'engagement de chacun, mais rien ne supporte cette énergie individuelle et collective à vouloir que les choses tiennent ensemble. Cette condition, dure mais peut-être libre, tragique mais parfois magique, constitue un enseignement sur l'importance d'une structure, son impact, son mode de présence et sur ce qu'elle peut faire émerger ou étouffer en termes d'énergie humaine...
L'importance de la structure est posée dans tous nos projets dès leur genèse. Nous ne travaillons jamais sur les questions de structure après avoir réfléchi au projet, mais en même temps. En tant qu'architecte, je pense qu'une structure doit affranchir l'usager, le libérer et non le limiter. Une structure a pour fonction principale de relier les gens tout en les détachant. C'est un système d'interaction passionnant. C'est pourquoi une structure est nécessairement en mouvement. Elle doit montrer qu'il n'y a pas de limite entre nous, ni en nous-même. Travailler l'architecture par la structure permet finalement de construire les liaisons et la cohésion du projet. Et cette structure ne doit rien affirmer sur la manière dont le monde tient et fonctionne. Selon moi, une structure doit nécessairement poser question.
Et dans un même temps, une structure permet de revenir à une forme de naïveté, à un archaïsme qui refuse la référence. Pour la réalisation de la Villa T, nous ne voulions pas ajouter de matière, de code ou de langage à la structure. Cette villa se comporte structurellement comme une tortue. La structure fait habiter, elle fait l'architecture. Et parallèlement, exprimée à l'état brut, la structure traduit une fragilité. Il en est de même de la Villa M situé sur les hauteurs de Beyrouth, sur le flanc d'une pente extrêmement raide. À la regarder depuis la route, on ne sait pas du tout comment cette maison est accrochée, ni comment elle tient en équilibre. Elle donne un sentiment de perpétuelle intranquillité et de risque. C'est important pour moi de ne pas rassurer par la structure, de ne pas tout exprimer. Sa part cachée, secrète, apporte aussi une lecture du monde.
Ainsi, chaque structure que nous concevons contient un grand potentiel d'évolutivité et de remise en question. Selon nous, une structure doit permettre le changement. Elle doit évoluer, s'adapter. C'est un système vivant. Ses mouvements sont internes, invisibles mais perpétuels. Pour la conception de la Villa T, nous avons considéré beaucoup de fluctuations pour calculer cette structure, car le coefficient de magnitude était élevé, le porte-à-faux, profond, et les panneaux de verre, de dimensions importantes.
Nous ne travaillons jamais la structure d'un projet de façon démonstrative. Nous cherchons toujours à exprimer un échappement et une forme de fragilité, d'inquiétude. Cela conduit à penser que l'on a besoin d'interdépendances. Une structure ne peut exister

seule, c'est un ensemble hétérogène. En architecture, elle représente un collectif, on oublie trop souvent cela. Elle n'est pas une entité qui fait autorité mais un ensemble délicat de fragments de construction, de points, de surfaces, d'articulations, d'assemblages en état de transmission. Elle porte en elle de nombreux paramètres liés au milieu, au sol, au vent, à la lumière, aux matériaux. Par essence, elle est à l'écoute du contexte existant. Elle doit répondre à des facteurs externes et internes de manière collective, mais elle n'est jamais finie ni figée. En cela, les choses deviennent intéressantes pour un architecte. Une structure tient les choses ensemble parce qu'elle est vivante. Elle permet à la vie humaine de se produire.

À quelle attitude de projet et à quelle relation à l'espace cette approche de la structure renvoie-t-elle ?

Quand j'aborde un projet, c'est par l'évidement. Je dessine d'abord un vide. J'essaie de mettre la personne, la rencontre, les potentiels d'échanges et de relations au premier plan. Je cherche à créer des « trous » pour qu'il se passe quelque chose. Creuser, plutôt que remplir, permet d'amener le lien et le silence. Évider me permet aussi de trouver cet état d'antériorité que je cherche pour chaque projet : comme si, fondamentalement, l'architecture était toujours un état antérieur, un état qui nous précède. L'architecture, en ce sens, est un recommencement, un tableau blanc déjà chargé.

Un creux permet de laisser la place. Un creux n'a pas de limite. Il offre les conditions de l'invitation. Il ouvre par l'intérieur. C'est une manière de regarder, de construire le monde et l'espace. C'est un moyen de chercher l'autre, une complémentarité, une imbrication. En cela, j'aime concevoir des espaces qui ne sont jamais finis, jamais terminés ni limités. J'aime imaginer des espaces qui attendent quelque chose. J'aime construire des flous. C'est ce qui me touche le plus.

Le site de Petra en Jordanie me parle beaucoup à ce titre, mais aussi l'église Saint-Pierre de Chaillot à Paris où il n'est question que de masse évidée traversée par la lumière. Cette lumière permet de casser les limites et de nous projeter dans un espace d'une autre nature. Le site de Petra nous enseigne comment un matériau brut peut devenir doux et habitable. Comment habiter et faire corps avec une falaise ? Qu'est ce qui compte le plus, la falaise ou ce qui a été creusé ? Ou les deux ensemble ? À Petra, il y a cette double situation très intense et, autour, le désert…

En cherchant à évider, je cherche à construire les conditions d'un milieu. J'entends, par milieu, l'espace de rencontre des énergies, des mouvements, l'espace de la compréhension, de la poésie et du silence. Au Liban, où il n'y a plus d'intérieur, cette quête est importante. Nous devons reconstruire des milieux, des possibilités de penser car nous n'avons plus de milieu.

Partir du milieu est une chance d'amener de l'illimité, de sortir de l'immédiat et de l'excitation, de ramener de la stabilité et de déplacer le débat. Construire des milieux est paradoxalement une forme de décentrement quand tout le monde focalise sur le remplissage ou le remplacement. C'est une occasion d'appartenir à quelque chose de plus grand pour échapper, de l'intérieur. En tant qu'architecte, j'aime travailler avec l'énergie existante des milieux. L'énergie est le flux même de l'espace, sa pulsation. J'ai toujours à cœur de la comprendre, de la toucher, de l'intensifier, de la révéler.

Pourquoi parle-t-on si peu d'énergie en architecture ? Hors de toute question formelle, culturelle ou matérielle, parler de l'énergie revient à parler de l'élémentaire, du primitif. Pour la conception de la Villa SC dans un village de la haute montagne libanaise, l'énergie a été le moteur du projet - à commencer par celle du client, si particulier, dont les pieds touchaient à peine le sol quand il se déplaçait. J'ai cherché à construire un espace à partir et autour de cette énergie individuelle et à la mélanger à celle, très puissante, du site, du vide. J'ai conçu cette maison comme une « cape » qui entoure un corps et une tête. Ce vêtement large a été imaginé comme un amplificateur de territoire. Quand on entre à l'intérieur de cette maison, le site paraît plus fort, plus intense, plus puissant. J'ai déjà ressenti ce phénomène dans le désert. Si on enfile un linge, une robe, alors on ressent encore plus le désert. Il s'agit d'un phénomène étrange, précisément parce qu'il est lié à la capacité d'une architecture à nous transformer. Dans le désert, l'architecture, c'est la robe autour de soi. Dans ce village de haute montagne, l'architecture est une grande cavité sensible, ouverte, poreuse, pierreuse.

Pourquoi le désert semble-t-il plus fort quand on enfile une robe ?

Peut-être parce qu'on est dénudé, dans un état élémentaire face à lui, donc réceptif à ce que le milieu agisse sur nous. Ensuite, la robe devient une entrée. Et cette entrée a le pouvoir de nous inclure et de nous relier. La robe, c'est l'espace d'échange, du passage de l'énergie. Elle permet cet échange, c'est une enveloppe respirante qui subitement nous met en lien avec un milieu.
La robe est aussi une manière de prendre conscience de la relation, de prendre conscience du désert et, ainsi, de dialoguer par le corps. Grâce à cette robe, on réalise qu'on est en lien, qu'on entre en échange avec un milieu. Une architecture peut avoir le même pouvoir que cette robe dont nous parlons. C'est un outil de conscience très puissant. Pour la Villa SC, l'architecture révèle deux présences simultanément, celle de l'homme et celle de la montagne. Cette simultanéité active la relation d'échange entre le site et le corps, chacun dans leur totalité.
C'est très difficile de décrire un paysage. On est très vite imprécis ou confus. Quoiqu'on dise, il nous échappe. Mais si, tout à coup, on y place une architecture, on focalise et on réalise finalement ce qu'il est. C'est en le précisant qu'on l'intensifie. Cette dimension est intéressante. Je crois que la précision permet de rendre présent. Elle permet de rendre présent quelque chose dont l'impact et la conscience sinon nous échapperaient. Cet état de présence par l'architecture procure une émotion incroyable. Peut-être parce que l'architecture nous permet de faire corps avec le paysage, de l'intérioriser, d'en capter et d'en absorber l'énergie profonde.
La robe dans le désert ou la maison en haute montagne nous placent dans le présent. Le fait d'entrer dans une architecture nous pose dans une situation active de relation, qui permet de concentrer toutes nos émotions et de les décupler. Au même titre qu'une architecture, un mot permet d'agrandir une situation et de la rendre plus forte. L'architecture agit sur nous comme un texte. Elle a ce pouvoir de nous détacher, de nous emporter tout en nous ancrant dans le sol. Tout comme la robe ou la maison, le mot incarne aussi cette possibilité de l'échange.
Je pense fondamentalement que les choses deviennent plus fortes quand l'humain est en situation de partage. C'est notre condition. L'acte de construire est avant tout un acte pour lier et chercher le point de rencontre entre l'individuel et le collectif. Cela renvoie également à une manière de penser l'espace par « stratifications ». Cette idée de *layers* touche en moi quelque chose de fondamental. Cela signifie que les choses ne s'arrêtent pas, ne se limitent pas mais qu'elles se superposent. C'est une dynamique de la perception.
Dans notre projet de requalification du quartier Bruneseau entre Paris et Ivry, cette question a été cruciale. Le site est très dense et intense. Nous ne voulions pas créer des rapports de frontalité ni d'immédiateté entre l'habitant et la ville. Cette intention modifie complètement l'idée même de façade. Dans la tour de logements que nous dessinons, les *layers* existent par l'intermédiaire de dispositifs spatiaux - un banc, un rebord, une baignoire, une rupture d'échelle. Ils permettent de donner une profondeur à la relation à l'extérieur et rendent ainsi possible une intériorité active. Ils créent les conditions d'un échange qu'un rapport trop direct, dans un tel contexte, n'aurait pas forcément permis. Ils permettent d'engendrer, de commencer une histoire là où il n'y a rien.
Nous avons exploré cela pour la Villa T près de Beyrouth, mais sous une tout autre forme. Quand on pénètre à l'intérieur du salon, le porte-à-faux de 13 mètres de la dalle en béton et le changement abrupt de hauteur sous plafond permettent de passer d'une situation resserrée, voire confinée, à un sentiment de pleine ouverture sur le vide. Sans utiliser de dispositif au sol ni de paroi, cette idée de *layers* est pourtant très sensible. La rupture d'échelle marque ici tout à la fois une transition et un changement d'état.

Quel recul avez-vous aujourd'hui sur votre double expérience, libanaise et française ?

Pour approcher cette question, il est important de revenir sur les différences fondamentales entre les situations française et libanaise. Je vais être volontairement un peu généraliste et forcer le trait afin de bien donner à comprendre les tendances qui sont en jeu dans ces deux parties du monde et qui ont, pour ma part, conduit à des expériences de projet tout à fait distinctes.
La France tout comme le reste de l'Europe est un pays largement industrialisé. Cette industrialisation de l'acte de construire et de produire est associée à une certaine vision collective et centralisatrice qui vise à protéger le plus grand nombre, à prévenir, anticiper, fabriquer massivement et rapidement, à développer, progresser. Les conséquences sur l'architecture et la ville sont bien sûr très importantes. L'urbanisme qui

en découle est un acte politique, d'intérêt public, relevant d'un cadre réglementé.
Tout comme la France, le Liban est dominé par l'économie de marché mais ce n'est pas un pays industrialisé. L'industrialisation comme manière de diriger, d'engendrer ou de contrôler n'est pas collectivement admise ni intégrée. L'état de guerre dans lequel nous sommes plongés depuis plus de quarante ans ne nous a pas permis de construire une vision partagée et collective du monde ni de la ville. Le gouvernement agit sans vision commune, sans projet de société. La ville de Beyrouth traduit parfaitement cette dynamique de court-terme. Dans ce contexte où le groupe ne peut pas exister, l'individu a pris le relais et son pouvoir est très fort. Sa marge de manœuvre est très importante car il n'a pas à se conformer à une vision collective. Il ne dépend pas d'un système où tout est pensé pour s'imbriquer et s'enchaîner, où le cadre est prédominant sur l'individu. Cette situation permet de vivre et d'agir beaucoup plus librement, de manière encore « artisanale ». Cela laisse une réelle capacité à l'individu d'intervenir dans la production, la fabrication et la création.
Du point de vue de l'acte de construire, on ne préfabrique pas au Liban et on coule le béton en place. De même, on ne subit aucun lobby industriel, ce qui est impensable en France ! Quant au poids des promoteurs, nous avons encore affaire à des individus et non à des groupes. Il est toujours possible de discuter et de négocier. Cela change tout. On peut donc travailler le projet autrement et concevoir tout ce qui le constitue. L'architecte peut pleinement profiter de ces marges de liberté. Cela signifie également qu'il doit tout anticiper car rien n'est vraiment systématisé, prévu ou rodé. Cela peut générer le pire comme le meilleur... De même, les règles sont là pour être discutées. Le pays n'est juridiquement pas assez précis pour imposer un cadre. En France, la précision des règles permet de limiter les dégâts, d'assurer l'équité, de maîtriser l'énergie, etc., mais elle constitue aussi un « format » du monde. Ces différences entre les deux pays sont fondamentales.

Quelles sont les conséquences de ces différences sur la pratique ?

Être architecte au Liban offre donc une latitude certaine. En effet, on peut s'impliquer dans toute la chaîne du projet et travailler de près avec les artisans. À l'inverse, dans le système français, les marges de liberté sont très réduites pour les architectes. La commande est très encadrée, l'urbanisme très fort, la pression de groupes et des lobbys est énorme, et la réglementation très rigide.
Quand j'ai travaillé en tant qu'urbaniste sur les projets de transformation du quartier de Brazza à Bordeaux ou de Bruneseau entre Paris et Ivry, j'ai eu la chance de pouvoir intervenir très en amont dans le premier cas et, dans le second, d'intervenir sur une situation tellement atypique - autour d'infrastructures, sur le périphérique, entre deux villes - que les promoteurs n'ont pas pu prendre les devants dès le début du projet. Dans les deux cas, on a dû s'écouter et avancer ensemble dans un travail d'échange et de négociation.
Pour le projet de Bordeaux, j'ai essayé de donner une vraie légitimité à ce qui relève de l'imprévu, d'ouvrir de nouvelles portes afin de constituer un quartier hors du modèle générique de la ZAC : un morceau de ville doté de différentes strates et échelles, dans lequel les habitants peuvent s'impliquer. J'ai notamment cherché à séquencer le plan de masse afin d'éviter des découpes en macro-lots, à varier les typologies de logement et à les confronter, à proposer un grand nombre de volumes capables - des surfaces de 5 mètres sous plafond laissées à la liberté d'aménager des habitants. J'ai pu opérer ainsi car j'étais très en amont du projet, au début de la chaîne de fabrication.
Où que je sois, je refuse d'être dans l'obligation de construire vite, je tiens à maîtriser les coûts de construction et les relations aux entreprises, et à revenir à ce que vaut vraiment la matière. C'est une attitude extrêmement difficile à tenir en France...
J'espère que les conditions de production de la ville en France vont changer. Dans la municipalité de Bordeaux, on commence à s'interroger sur le fait de freiner les autorisations de permis de construire pour réfléchir autrement, construire moins et moins vite. C'est encourageant.

Comment abordez-vous la question du « faire », qui redevient centrale pour les habitants ?

En France, l'acte de faire été confisqué notamment par cette croyance dans l'industrialisation de la société dont les produits, facilités et services se sont répandus dans nos vies et particulièrement en milieu urbain. L'acte de faire est devenu un objet théorique, on l'a intellectualisé faute de pouvoir s'en saisir physiquement. Or, il semble qu'on revienne tous aujourd'hui à ce besoin de sentir, de toucher, de s'impliquer dans la fabrication de l'espace physique, qu'il s'agisse d'habitat ou d'espace public. La crise sanitaire que nous traversons, les empêchements et frustrations qui l'accompagnent nous font percevoir la finitude du monde. Nous la sentons physiquement. On va devoir accepter cela. L'Occident ne peut plus continuer de croire en la modernité. Cette période de transition est très intéressante.

Qu'il s'agisse de l'habitat ou de l'aménagement urbain, je pense que l'on doit revenir à une visibilité de la chaîne de production. Pour la biennale Agora à Bordeaux en 2014, j'ai visité un site d'exploitation de carrière à Ouagadougou où toute la chaîne de fabrication de l'espace public était visible. Chaque habitant participe en effet à sa production et sait précisément d'où vient la matière qu'il travaille et comment elle a été transformée. Chacun a une conscience très forte de la ville, de l'artisanat à l'échelle urbaine. Chacun appartient à un système de création partagé. Cette question, très théorisée en France, n'est pas assez prise au sérieux dans la pratique. Je pense que le rapport à l'appropriation, à la durabilité, à l'évolutivité de la ville et de l'architecture dépend essentiellement de la position que l'on donne aux habitants et citoyens. Cela signifie renoncer à une certaine culture du contrôle et de la maîtrise pour donner de la liberté aux habitants et leur faire confiance.

Cette situation nouvelle renvoie à un autre point très important aujourd'hui : l'expérience collective de l'imprévisible. La pandémie mondiale que nous traversons a en effet touché tous les pays, et notamment les démocraties politiquement stables où, très profondément, les priorités semblent s'être déplacées. En cela, la crise sanitaire nous met tous sur un pied d'égalité et c'est très intéressant. Nous partageons à présent cette conscience commune que l'on ne maîtrise rien, qu'on le veuille ou non. Il en découle de par le monde une soif particulière d'universalité, d'émotions simples dans l'espace physique. En effet, la peur, l'angoisse, les frustrations et le manque changent les priorités de chacun et les manières de voir.

Les longues années de guerre que nous avons vécues au Liban ont très vite fait comprendre à la population que l'imprévu était une chance. Une chance de s'en sortir. Chacun a pu saisir, dès qu'une occasion s'est présentée, la possibilité de travailler et vivre autrement. Le moindre renversement a pu se transformer en opportunité. Et aujourd'hui, cette notion d'imprévisibilité relie très fortement tous les Libanais. Tout le monde a intégré la culture du plan B, la culture du retournement. L'imprévu nous apprend qu'une nouvelle donne, aussitôt qu'on l'accepte, peut faire partie de notre quotidien et devenir porteuse de projet.

En France, on ne pense pas encore qu'un imprévu, un « accident », puisse être une chance. Toute l'organisation de la ville et de la société est orientée pour éviter les situations inattendues. Mais aujourd'hui, nous faisons face à l'imprévu le plus puissant que nous ayons jamais connu… Et nous sommes tout à coup collectivement liés à cette même chose que représente la conscience de l'imprévu comme une réelle donnée dans nos vies.

Nous entrons sans doute dans une nouvelle ère, celle du présent. Et c'est une chose nouvelle pour toutes les générations d'après-guerre. L'angoisse est pour l'instant mondiale. Les gouvernements essayent de calmer les populations mais, au fond, on a tous changé. On ne pourra plus jamais vivre ni penser comme avant.

La période si étrange que nous vivons aujourd'hui est intéressante du point de vue du territoire. Je pense qu'un milieu prend une importance plus grande en temps d'incertitude. Aujourd'hui, nous approchons le paysage, le climat, le ciel autrement car nous vivons un danger. Un espace dégage une énergie particulièrement forte quand l'homme ressent de l'angoisse ou de la joie… Je pense que nous expérimentons aujourd'hui collectivement des dimensions tout à fait nouvelles en termes d'ouverture, de vide et de milieu.

Acknowledgements

My profound thanks to all the people who helped me with the realisation of this book:

Roger Akoury
Karine Dana
Sebastian Redecke
Muhammad Mahdi
Shaha Raphael
Toufic Dagher
Mohammad Ali Ahmad
Jihane Abou Ghazali
Bassam Feghali
Helen Korban
Henriette Mueller-Stahl
Silke Nalbach

About the Authors

Karine Dana, an architect by training, works as an architectural journalist and videographer. Due to this dual perspective she provides through writing and the act of filming, the Lacaton & Vassal, YTAA, and 51N4E offices call upon her services regularly in the context of competitions, research projects and exhibitions. Her long-term collaboration with the architect Youssef Tohme began in 2014 with the book *Intensive Beyrouth*, published by Éditions Norma.
Karine Dana's work is driven by a constant preoccupation: to capture as precisely and delicately as possible what space produces through territories, both between people and within them.

Sebastian Redecke is an architect. After an upbringing in Brussels and Göttingen, and studies at the TU Braunschweig and the University of Rome, he worked in various architectural offices in Munich and Berlin. Since 1990 he has been editor of the architecture journal *Bauwelt* in Berlin and is the author or co-editor of several books. His primary areas of interest include contemporary architecture and urban planning in Berlin and Paris.

About the Architect

Youssef Tohme and YTAA—Youssef Tohme Architects and Associates
Youssef Tohme graduated from the Paris-Villemin School of Architecture in 1997 and taught theory at the same school in 1999. Between 2000 and 2006 he worked in several Parisian offices. Concurrently, he developed personal projects in Lebanon, including the Campus of Innovation, Economy and Sport in Beirut (USJ) in association with 109 Architectes.
In 2008, he founded Y.Tohme/Architects in Beirut. Together with a team of Lebanese architects, he sought to articulate his theoretical and technical research with his practice in architectural and urban projects. According to Youssef Tohme, "*Social diversity, freedom, in-betweenness, inhabitation, silence, the unexpected and the landscape are all themes that the agency studies in order to develop its projects. The architecture that is meaningful to us speaks of the world in which we live.*" The focus tends to be on the structure of habitats, relationships, uses, atmosphere, appropriation rather than on houses, such as Villa T, Villa SC, Villa M, etc.
Internationally, the office has already completed or is currently working on a number of cultural, residential and urban buildings, such as MARe, The Museum of Recent Art in Bucharest, delivered in 2018, or the Cambridge School also in Romania.
2012, YTAA—Youssef Tohme Architects and Associates wins the urban planning competition organised by Bordeaux City Council for the redevelopment of the Brazza Nord district.
2013, Youssef Tohme is appointed curator of the September 2014 edition of Agora, a biennial architecture, urban planning and design event held in Bordeaux, focusing on the question of public space.
2015, Youssef Tohme is awarded the "médaille de l'urbanisme" by the French Academy of Architecture for his work in the city of Bordeaux.
2016, the YTAA agency is selected for the project to construct of 120 housing units on the Île de Nantes, including an 11-floor timber-frame tower.
January 2018, Youssef Tohme is admitted to the French Academy of Architecture.
March 2019, the office, as part of the Nouvel R consortium, is announced as the winner of the "Bruneseau" competition linking Paris to the suburb of Ivry.
YTAA will build a 180-metre-high apartment block overlooking Paris.
In April 2019, the agency wins the "Îlot sur le Parc" competition for a mixed programme in the centre of Marseille.
Alongside these projects, Youssef Tohme continues giving lectures in several countries to explore themes that inform the work of the YTAA office.
Youssef Tohme and his friend Roger Akoury have been joint partners of YTAA since 2012.

Illustration Credits

Toufic Dagher
p. 22/23, p. 32/33, p. 39, p. 61, p. 62/63, p. 65, p. 68, p. 69,
p. 71, p. 84, p. 85 bottom, p. 86/87, p. 140/141, p. 142, p. 151,
p. 180, p. 182, p. 185, p. 188/189, p. 191, p. 198/199
Cosmin Dragomir
p. 72/73, p. 75, p. 76, p. 77, p. 80, p. 81
Joe Kesrouani
p. 34/35, p. 36/37, p. 41, p. 43, p. 44, p. 46, p. 47
Shaha Raphael
p. 88, p. 91, p. 92, p. 95, p. 96, p. 101, p. 102, p. 107, p. 108, p. 113,
p. 116, p. 119, p. 122
Ieva Saudargaite
p. 6/7, p. 8, p. 12/13, p. 14, p. 15 top, p. 16/17, p. 18/19, p. 20,
p. 24 top, p. 26/27, p. 30, p. 40, p. 56/57, p. 59, p. 60, p. 64,
p. 126/127, p. 128, p. 129, p. 133, p. 134, p. 136/137, p. 139,
p. 143, p. 144/145, p. 148/149, p. 152, p. 153, p. 154, p. 178/179,
p. 186, p. 187, p. 192/193, p. 194, p. 197, p. 201

All other illustrations